UTB

W0361549

Eine Arbeitsgemeinschaft der Verlage

Böhlau Verlag · Wien · Köln · Weimar
Verlag Barbara Budrich · Opladen · Toronto
facultas.wuv · Wien
Wilhelm Fink · München
A. Francke Verlag · Tübingen und Basel
Haupt Verlag · Bern
Verlag Julius Klinkhardt · Bad Heilbrunn
Mohr Siebeck · Tübingen
Nomos Verlagsgesellschaft · Baden-Baden
Ernst Reinhardt Verlag · München · Basel
Ferdinand Schöningh · Paderborn · München · Wien · Zürich
Eugen Ulmer Verlag · Stuttgart
UVK Verlagsgesellschaft · Konstanz, mit UVK/Lucius · München
Vandenhoeck & Ruprecht · Göttingen · Bristol
vdf Hochschulverlag AG an der ETH Zürich

StandardWissen Lehramt

Die Bände zur Didaktik des Englischen werden herausgegeben von Engelbert Thaler

Bislang sind erschienen in der Reihe:

Teaching Grammar von J.-U. Keßler/A. Plesser (UTB 3448)
Task-Supported Language Learning von A. Müller-Hartmann/M. Schocker-von Ditfurth (UTB 3336)
Teaching English Literature von E. Thaler (UTB 2897)
Computer-assisted Language Learning von K. Heim/M. Ritter (UTB 3334)

Engelbert Thaler

Teaching English with Films

Ferdinand Schöningh

Der Autor:

Engelbert Thaler, Prof. Dr. phil. habil., ist Professor für die Didaktik des Englischen an der Universität Augsburg. Nach dem Lehramtsstudium arbeitete er 20 Jahre als Gymnasiallehrer für Englisch und Sozialkunde. Er habilitierte sich an der Ludwig-Maximilians-Universität München über offene Lernarrangements im Fremdsprachenunterricht. Seine Publikationen befassen sich neben mediendidaktischen Themen u.a. mit unterrichtsmethodologischen Fragen (Balanced Teaching), literaturdidaktischen Zugängen und kulturkundlichen Aspekten. Thaler ist auch Herausgeber von Schulbüchern, Fachzeitschriften und Unterrichtsreihen.

Online-Angebote oder elektronische Ausgaben sind erhältlich unter **www.utb-shop.de**

Bibliografische Information der Deutschen Nationalbibliothek

Die Deutsche Nationalbibliothek verzeichnet diese Publikation in der Deutschen Nationalbibliografie; detaillierte bibliografische Daten sind im Internet über http://dnb.d-nb.de abrufbar.

(Verlag Ferdinand Schöningh GmbH & Co. KG, Jühenplatz 1, D-33098 Paderborn)

Internet: www.schoeningh.de

Printed in Germany.
Herstellung: Ferdinand Schöningh, Paderborn
Einbandgestaltung: Atelier Reichert, Stuttgart

UTB-Band-Nr: 3946
ISBN 978-3-8252-3946-6

Vorwort zur Reihe

StandardWissen Lehramt – Studienbücher für die Praxis

Wie das gesamte Bildungswesen wird sich auch die künftige Lehramtsausbildung an Kompetenzen und Standards orientieren. Damit rückt die Frage in den Vordergrund, was Lehrkräfte wissen und können müssen, um ihre berufliche Praxis erfolgreich zu bewältigen. Das Spektrum reicht von fachlichen Fähigkeiten über Diagnosekompetenzen bis hin zu pädagogisch-psychologischem Wissen, um Lehren als Unterstützung zur Selbsthilfe und Lernen als eigenaktiven Prozess fassen zu können.

Kompetenzen werden nicht in einem Zug erworben; Lehrerbildung umfasst nicht nur das Studium an einer Hochschule, sondern ebenso das Referendariat und die Berufsphase. Die Reihe StandardWissen Lehramt bei UTB bietet daher Lehramtsstudierenden, Referendaren, Lehrern in der Berufseinstiegsphase und Fortbildungsteilnehmern jenes wissenschaftlich abgesicherte Know-How, das sie im Rahmen einer neu orientierten Ausbildung wie auch später in der Schule benötigen. Fachdidaktische und pädagogisch-psychologische Themen werden gleichermaßen in dieser Buchreihe vertreten sein – einer Basisbibliothek für alle Lehramtsstudierenden, Referendare, Lehrerinnen und Lehrer.

Contents

SPECIAL FORMATS

CONCLUSION

Introduction

Importance of movies

Watching movies and going to to the cinema play an important part in people's lives. Our dress code, hairstyle, way of speaking, eating habits, attitudes to family life, and understanding of the world are constantly influenced by the film industry. Whether you adhere to the *modeling theory* (people imitate TV / film models and adopt their patterns of behaviour), or the *cultural norms theory* (the media establish the standards which define acceptable behaviour in our society), information from films, television and mass media in general has impacted enormously on how we live our daily lives. This fact should also be reflected in the English language classroom.

Critique of movies

Cultural critics, of course, may object that films are just part of popular or mass culture. They are nothing but commodities whose sole purpose is to be sold, aimed merely at manipulating consumers, designed with pre-digested formulas and calculated effects, lacking in artistic beauty, not concerned with truth. From this viewpoint, popular culture has eclipsed high culture, and the simulated has replaced the real. Moreover watching TV and films is said to make people fat, stupid, and aggressive (Spitzer 2005).

Impact of popular culture

Other scholars, however, take a more unbiased view. Steven Johnson (2005), for example, argues that today's popular culture is actually making us smarter. Over the past thirty years, it has grown more complex, become intellectually more demanding, and is improving our society in terms of intelligence and creativity. Whereas earlier TV programmes relied on simplified narrative and human relationships, modern series improve the audience's cognitive skills by using "multiple threading", inserting numerous intertextual references, increasing the number of characters, but reducing the number of "flashing arrows", i.e. narrative clues which help the viewers understand the plot; thus they require the audience to pay more attention to background information if they do not wish to get lost. Sitcoms and drama programmes promote emotional intelligence as well as the understanding of social signals. In particular children's films like Toy Story or Shrek, Johnson claims, have reached a level of cognitive and social complexity to make even adults feel wonderfully entertained.

Flynn effect

In addition, Johnson recognizes a connection between our increasingly complex popular culture on the one hand and the so-called Flynn effect on the other. This phenomenon named after its inventor James Flynn, says that there has been a substantial and long-sustained increase in intelligence test scores (IQ) in industrial countries since 1890. According to these studies, our pupils and students are not becoming less and less intelligent – as some people would like to suggest – but rather their intelligence levels are rising – and the new media make us smarter. Based on this belief, some advocates of Film-based Language Learning (FBLL) no longer need to suffer an inferiority complex when making use of films at school.

Intention and structure

This book intends to help those professional people when teaching English with films. As it is an introduction, it aims to look at all the main areas of FBLL in a user-friendly way, but refrains from probing too deeply into each field. The book consists of three parts, comprising 15 chapters, so that university teachers may – if they wish to – devote one weekly meeting to each chapter, covering the entire contents in one term. Being a bit longer, the first two chapters may be taught in three or four meetings, whereas two of the shorter chapters (long formats, conclusion) can be covered in one meeting each. The first part (*basis*) tries to answer the questions as to what FBLL and film literacy are, and why, when, where, and for what films should be employed in foreign language classrooms. The second part discusses the major *genres* that our students could come across in film classes (short, medium, long, special formats). The final part (*conclusion*) tries to round off the topic by presenting ways of assessing pupils as well as encouraging a Balanced FBLL.

New type of textbook

Teaching English with Films gives its readers a brief and reader-friendly introduction to an emerging field of study. A didactically reflected and consistent structure, several graphical elements, a focus on the essential aspects and a – hopefully – clear style aim at giving the reader a quick and comprehensive survey of the new field. It is written for university students (and their lecturers), practising teachers and anybody interested in making films a rewarding resource in English language classrooms.

In this book every chapter starts with an awareness-raising, pre-reading question, which often makes readers reflect on their own personal experiences. That is important, because the teacher development and the concept of reflective teaching have to take the (future) teacher's learning biography into consideration. All the chapters about genre are consistently structured into three parts: theory, methodology and lessons. A wide number of example lesson plans for various levels are meant to put the theoretical and methodological argumentation into practice. They have been tried out by teachers and teacher trainees (with special thanks to the participants of my *Hauptseminar*!). Readers are invited to use them in their courses at school, university or teacher training seminars – and send back their experiences to me: Your feedback is always welcome!

Basis

1 Film-Based Language Learning

What is your favourite film (clip)? Have you seen *The German Coast Guard* yet?

1.1 Sample Clip

A short commercial video may indicate what great potential films can have, and to what manifold uses they can be put.

The German Coast Guard

In this hilarious Berlitz commercial, a young German coastguard is being given instructions in his new job by an elderly man. As soon as the experienced man leaves, the trainee receives a distress call from an English boat:
"We are sinking!"
After a pause the coastguard asks:
"What are you sinking (thinking) about?"
http://www.youtube.com/watch?v=8vBn2_ia8zM

Example: Potential of films

Although this funny clip just lasts 40 seconds and does not contain very much language, it can be employed in many areas of TEFL (Teaching English as a Foreign Language), for example:

- Pronunciation: problems with pronouncing /th/
- Linguistics: minimal pairs like thinking / sinking
- Grammar: present progressive for actions happening right now
- Mediation: putting the first part (German instructions) into English
- Speaking: discussing the source of humour
- Global language: English as world language in sea traffic
- Intercultural learning: misunderstandings based on different languages
- Advertising: form, function and success of Berlitz commercial

1.2 History

A century of FBLL

The first article on using audio-visual media in classrooms was published in *English Journal* in 1913 (Baddock 1990: 147). However, this hardly had any impact on teaching for the next four or five decades. Things began to change in the 1960s. McLuhan's thesis of the *global village* sparked growing media awareness, the field of film adaptations developed rapidly, and the rise of semiotics helped film theory to obtain an academically accepted status.

Audio-visual media have been employed in foreign language classrooms for more than fifty years now, though to a limited extent. It has been common usage either to show film versions of famous novels and plays after the literary piece has been analysed in close reading, or to grant students 90 minutes of entertainment with a popular Hollywood movie before the beginning of holidays – without any specific teaching objectives.

The growing importance of mass media and popular culture is being studied by several academic disciplines. In the field of foreign language learning the concepts of *media literacy* and *intercultural learning* have drawn scholars' attention to English language films, which open windows to foreign cultures, using cinematic devices worthy of being analysed.

Cinderella paradox

Yet, in spite of a growing acceptance of film and video in academic discourse (e.g. Baddock 1996; Lütge 2012; Sherman 2003; Stempleski/Tomalin 2001; Surkamp 2004; Thaler 2007), and a broad popular appeal of movies with teenagers, films and other audio-visual media still lead a sort of Cinderella existence in classrooms. 100 years after the publication of the first article on films in education, films are still used to a limited degree: "rarely" by 78% of the teachers surveyed, "never" by 16%, "frequently" only by 6% (Thaler 2007).

1.3 Technology

Up to the 1970s, audio-visual technology had made showing a film in class a rather painstaking and time-consuming adventure, allowing straight-through viewing only. In 1969, Sony introduced a prototype for the first widespread video cassette, and with the launching of Sony's Betamax (1975) and JVC's VHS (1976), vide-

Abb. 1 | Bell & Howell movie projector (1934)

otape finally moved into the mass market. This videotape technology offered more methodological options for teachers, e.g. manipulating the presentation of a film (pause button, rewind etc.).

Impact of DVD

The invention of the DVD turned out to be an even greater step forward for language teachers. The Digital Versatile Disc (or Digital Video Disc), an optical disc storage media format, developed by Sony and Philips in 1995, increased versatility enormously: apart from better auditory as well as visual quality and higher storage capacity, teachers profit, in particular, from:

- different language versions ➤ English, German, French etc.
- subtitles ➤ facilitating listening comprehension, promoting reading skills, enabling cross-lingual language teaching (e.g. English soundtrack & German subtitles)
- direct scene access ➤ no time-consuming forward / rewind to get to the right spot, enabling sandwich techniques (skipping scenes)
- extras (bonus materials) ➤ fostering media literacy (background information on cinematic devices, interviews with directors / actors / cameramen)

Audio-visual materials can also be stored on a CD-ROM, which is an acronym of "compact disc read-only memory". It is popularly used to distribute computer software, including games and multimedia applications, though any data can be stored.

The advent of the Internet has made access to films even more comfortable. Video sharing websites like YouTube offer all kinds of audio-visual formats anytime for free (for legal issues such as copyright see Henseler / Möller / Surkamp 2011: 252ff.).

Internet

1.4 Rationale

An audio-visual text appeals to cognitive, communicative, personal, and emotional dimensions.

It can serve as an information text (speaking and writing about the film) as well as an instrumental text (language learning with the film) (Liebelt 1989: 251). In particular, it is suitable for understanding and using spoken language – supported by para-linguistic aids of interpretation (listening with one's eyes). This definitely is a vital benefit because colloquial, interactive language use still plays a minor role in language classrooms. As logistical barriers can now be overcome more and more easily (English language TV channels, Internet, DVD rental stores, growing supply, cheaper DVD offers), the value of films as a resource for learning seems beyond doubt: "Video ... can be used with great pleasure and profit" (Sherman 2001: 1).

Studying the relevant references (e.g. Leitzke-Ungerer 2009; Lütge 2012; Sherman 2003; Stempleski/Tomalin 2001; Zerweck 2004; Thaler 2010), one regularly encounters the following arguments for making use of audio-visual materials in the foreign language classroom.

Arguments for FBLL

Arguments for Films in TEFL	
Rationale	*References*
Popularity and motivation	"Video is today's medium" (Sherman 2001:2).
Audio-visual appeal	"If it moves they will watch it" (Andy Warhol).
Authenticity	"People want access to the world of English-language media" (Sherman 2001:2).
Personal relevance	"There is no biography without the cinema" (Hellmuth Karasek).
Receptive competences (listening, viewing)	"To learn to speak to people they must see and hear people speaking to each other" (Sherman 2001:14).

Arguments for Films in TEFL	
Productive competences (speaking, writing, mediating)	"Media-transmitted content, in particular, evokes the need to think, feel, judge, and act on one's own" (Erdmenger 1989:130).
Intertextual-literary competences	film on book or book on film – Surkamp (2004), Nold/Steffenhagen (2004)
Intercultural learning	Film as "moving picture book" (Sherman 2001:3)
Media / film literacy	"... the formal, functional and aesthetic categories of media formats ..." (Thaler 2007).

Acceptance by teachers

Films are popular with teenagers – and they are accepted by teachers. In an empirical study, two thirds of the teachers questioned assessed FBLL as "very positive" or "positive", around 30% viewed it "neutrally", only two teachers voted for "more negative than positive", the category of "very negative" was never ticked off (Thaler 2007).

CEF

Reviewing all these arguments for the use of films in language learning, it comes as no surprise that European, national and federal curricula have integrated films. The Common European Framework of Reference for Languages (CEF), for example, provides an illustrative scale for watching TV and film (Council of Europe 2001: Chapter 4.4.2.3).

CEF: Watching TV and Film	
C2	As C1
C1	Can follow films employing a considerable degree of slang and idiomatic usage.
B2	Can understand most TV news and current affairs programmes. Can understand documentaries, live interviews, talk shows, plays and the majority of films in standard dialect.
B1	Can understand a large part of many TV programmes on topics of personal interest such as interviews, short lectures, and news reports when the delivery is relatively slow and clear. Can follow many films in which visuals and action carry much of the storyline, and which are delivered clearly in straightforward language. Can catch the main points in TV programmes on familiar topics when the delivery is relatively slow and clear.

A2	Can identify the main point of TV news items reporting events, accidents etc. where the visual supports the commentary. Can follow changes of topic of factual TV news items, and form an idea of the main content.
A1	No descriptor

1.5 Formats

Classification by length

Audio-visual media may be classified according to genre or length. The latter makes clear that there are not only full-length feature films to be used for teaching but also shorter and medium formats, which, due to their compactness, are often easier to exploit in class.

Film Formats	
Types	*Examples*
Short forms (5 seconds – 5 minutes)	music videos, sketches, TV news, speeches, weather reports, commercials, interviews, trailers, Internet videos
Medium forms (20 – 45 minutes)	drama series, (live-action or animated) sitcoms, soap operas, talk shows, game shows, documentaries, educational films
Long forms (90+ minutes)	(live-action or animated) feature films, live coverage of national events, sports matches / tournaments

1.6 Selection

Variety of genres

The preceding table suggests a question which is of great importance for the success of FBLL: Which film should be selected for a special purpose? Feature films, documentaries and TV programmes are certainly the formats which are used most frequently and are also recommended explicitly in official guidelines. However, smaller genres such as TV news, weather forecasts, interviews, speeches, commercials, or clippings of medium formats like talk shows, sports programmes, or game shows should not be neglected. Against the background of variety and a spiral approach, a number of different genres should be made use of – regularly, repeatedly, progressing in difficulty.

Sources

By now there is a wealth of audio-visual materials on the market. The sources which are most relevant for language teachers are:

- DVDs: for sale or rental
- TV programmes: English language channels
- Film publishing companies' brochures: e. g. Lingua Video
- Websites: e. g. BBC or YouTube
- Coursebook publishers: film sections integrated into textbook or additional film materials

Criteria

The question teachers then have to answer is which of the various films available are actually suitable for their students. They may be guided in the process of selection by these criteria – with the right column indicating possible problems (Thaler 2012: 171f.):

Criteria of Selection

Criterion	*Problem areas*
Auditory features	• background noise • poor sound quality • multiple speakers • people speaking at the same time • use of unfamiliar accents • people speaking too quickly • complex syntax • elaborate style • abstract topic • argumentative und expository text formats • long film
Visual features	• lack of coherence • non-linear presentation • information given only implicitly • many scenes containing sex or violence
Relation between sound and image	• great language density (a lot of language per scene) • little visual support for spoken text • lack of correspondence between sound and image
Relevance	• topic of little relevance for students • topic unrelated to their interests, reality
Methodology	• lack of accompanying teaching suggestions • lack of didactic or thematic relevance

1.7 Presentation

5 modes

After selecting the right material, the question arises as to how to present it. In particular with medium and long formats, there are five general modes to choose from (Thaler 2008). As each of them displays both specific strengths and weaknesses, the decision should be based on the film itself, the objectives intended, the time available, the students' level ... and the principle of *variatio delectat*.

Major Modes of Film Presentation

Mode of presentation	*Description*
Straight through approach	Presenting the whole film in one sitting, without interruption
Segment approach	Presenting the whole film in separate segments (ca. 15'), successive viewing in several lessons
Sandwich approach	Showing selected scenes, summarizing deleted scenes (telling)
Clip approach	Presenting one scene / sequence only, e.g. beginning of feature film
Mixed approach	Combining some of the four major approaches in various constellations

1.8 Activities

Closed and open

When it comes to actually working with audio-visual materials in class, one can choose from a multitude of activities (Bredella 2004; Burwitz-Melzer 2004; Grau 2004; Gymnich 2004; Landesbildstelle Südbayern 2000; Lütge 2012; Stempleski/Tomalin 2001; Weißling/Yareham 2001 – also see chapter 2!). On the one hand, there are (rather closed) exercises, e.g. checking listening-viewing comprehension via questions, right / wrong statements, gapped dialogues, or matching quote and character (*Who said what?*). On the other, (more open) tasks such as creating a film script, writing a film response journal, staging a press conference, or producing a film leave the students more room for imagination and creation (Thaler 2007 – also see chapter 2!).

PWP

Apart from the degree of openness, activities may also be classified according to the phase they are employed in: pre-viewing, while-viewing, and post-viewing activities (see chapters 2 – 13).

1.9 Places

In & out

As far as the place of learning is concerned, films can be used in and out of the classroom, with various ways of combining the two venues being possible. Several arguments speak for a stronger focus on FBLL beyond the classroom: time pressure, promoting students' autonomy, and the observation that learners need a certain period of time for tuning in, in order to adjust to the foreign language and be able to process the target language film communication.

Beyond the classroom

The following – real or virtual – learning spaces are, at least partially, located outside the classroom (Thaler 2010):

- Project work: Within a longer time frame, students working in groups deal with various aspects of a topic. For example, they may create a movie magazine or compare an original film with its remake.
- Guided movie afternoon: Guided by tasks given in a preceding lesson, students watch a current movie in the local cinema.
- Blended FBLL: A film is watched at home and later presented in class.
- English language channels: Teachers should repeatedly remind their students that by now, several cable channels offer movies in the original. Moreover, the two-channel signal processor system allows you to switch from the dubbed to the original form of a foreign film.
- DVD lending library: A school or class library need not be restricted to printed material. Design, organization and funding of such an audio-visual rental store may be similar to those of a convential library. Evaluation sheets, which are filled in with students' comments, promote writing skills und help classmates to select suitable films.
- Visit to a film studio: To cast a glance behind the scenes, a project week or excursion day may be used to discover a film studio. For example, the Bavaria Studios in Munich offer a

guided tour plus a simulation of a scene in a blockbuster movie, with the students being able to take over the lead roles.

- Electronic exchanges: An E-mail-exchange project with an English-speaking class abroad may focus on a certain film, e.g. Freddie Frinton's New Year's Eve sketch *Dinner For One*, which is cult film in some European countries, yet hardly known in Great Britain. Electronic exchanges on selected Hollywood movies can also be organized via chat channels, forums or videoconferencing.
- Doing a WebQuest: This Internet-based application, which was invented by Bernie Dodge in 1995 and consists of six stages (introduction – task – information sources – process – guidance – conclusion), combines autonomy and guidance by using Internet data rather than looking for them. You can resort to ready-made WebQuests online on the topic of film or selected movie hits, or use suitable templates to create your own *FilmQuest*.
- Producing a movie: The most creative challenge probably lies in shooting your own film (see chapter 2).
- Making a vlog: The production of (short) films can also be organised on a regular basis by setting up a vlog (video & blog). The whole course or just a few individuals operate a website which adds new vlogs from time to time.

Abb. 2 | Dinner For One (classical New Year's Eve sketch)

1.10 Levels

Progression of levels

Simple forms like weather forecasts are suitable even for beginners in order to make them familiar with the medium. More elaborate short forms like commercials can facilitate and prepare the usage of long forms with advanced classes. Feature films and TV programmes are mentioned again and again in official documents (see above). Taking the principle of progression seriously, however, one should use shorter films with beginners and intermediate students, or insert regular comprehension checks with longer films. If you really intend to work with feature films profoundly, it is necessary to lay the foundations in lower classes with shorter audiovisual materials (Staatsinstitut 2005: 227, also see Henseler / Möller / Surkamp 2011: 24ff, proposal for a curriculum, as well as Lütge 2012: 107ff.).

Difficulty levels

To help you decide which film is appropriate for which level, the following table mentions several characteristics of a film: The ones in the second column suggest a usage of the film in more advanced classrooms, those in the third column are linked to lower levels.

Levels of Difficulty

Criterion	*Higher level*	*Lower level*
1. Genre	• Abstract text • Argumentative and expository types (e.g. docus) • Unfamiliar genre	• Concrete text • Narrative types (e. g. animated fairy tale) • Familiar genre
2. Complexity	• Complex syntax • Elaborated style • Complicated grammar • Unclear deixis	• Short main clauses • Clear references • Simple words and structures
3. Comprehensibility	• Noise • Many speakers • Simultaneuous speaking • Phonetic reductions • Unfamilar accents • High speed of talking	• Suitable, non-disturbing background sounds • Clear pronunciation • Slow talking speed • Standard pronunciation • One or two speakers
4. Language quantity	• A lot of spoken language per scene (e. g. talk shows)	• Little spoken language • Bilingual clips (e. g. English – German)
5. Exploitability	• Difficulties with designing suitable tasks	• Suitability for creating simple, clear exercises
6. Pedagogical suitability	• Mature content (violence, sex, drug abuse, profanity, impudence) • Motion picture rating system: not suitable for younger audiences	• Movie rating system: suitable for all

7. Relevance	• Lack of individual reference points	• Familiar environment • Interesting topics
8. Length	• Full-length feature films	• Short, self-contained clip
9. Sound-vision-relation	• Divergency between vision and sound • Little visual support of spoken language (e. g. TV news)	• Sound-vision congruity • Substantial visual support (e. g. weather forecast with map)
10. Discourse	• Lack of coherence • Non-linear line of narrative • Implicit information	• Clear structure • Chronological order • Accentuation of key scenes • Explicit information
11. Quality	• Low resolution (image quality) • Unclear sound	• High image quality • Good sound
12. Materials	• Lack of additional tasks, texts, background information	• Accompanying materials • Transcript available • Literary adaptation

Adapting difficulty

Even a film graded as difficult can be reduced to a lower student level by adapting the learning environment. The following suggestions make working with films easier:

- pre-viewing activities, e. g. introduction to topic, anticipating the content, pre-teaching key vocabulary
- specifying the purpose of viewing
- asking for global comprehension only
- repeated viewing of the same scene
- focusing on one code, e. g. silent viewing
- showing short scenes only
- limited number of questions for a short sequence
- chronological order of questions
- using closed formats for checking comprehension
- gapped texts with aids like indicating the number of letters
- pair or group work
- viewing aids: film observation sheets, how-to-write (a film review) scaffolds, language support lists (Lütge 2012: 34ff., Tepe 2004)

1.11 Problems

5 conflicts

In spite of the great didactic potential of audio-visual media, there are several problems which should not be ignored (Thaler 2008). The following table summarizes five conflicts – and possible ways to overcome them.

Time conflict

First a film is long, a lesson, however, is short. A 90-minute Hollywood blockbuster cannot be shown in its entirety – and worked on – in a 45-minute slot.

Language conflict

A second conflict results from the linguistic complexity and density of the film on the one hand and the students' restricted language competences on the other. Fast talking, background noises, disturbing music, colloquialisms, or clashes between words and action impair decoding capacities and result in frustration. "It demands higher language ability than any language student has ... Students switch off mentally as soon as they realise they can't follow the plot" (Baddock 1996: 4).

Reception conflict

A third conflict, the one between listening and viewing, arises when subtitles are switched on. When both modes of reception are appealed to, "the eye is more powerful than the ear" (Sherman 2001: 16), i.e. viewers tend to focus on the written inserts and neglect listening comprehension. Depending on the teacher's objectives, soundtrack and subtitles can be combined in three different ways, which display both benefits and drawbacks. English soundtrack plus English subtitles facilitate comprehension, promote reading skills rather than listening skills though. German subtitles make understanding an English film easier and may also be used for cross-lingual analysis; yet they focus the eye on the German text and restrain listening. German soundtrack plus English subtitles also lend themselves to L1-L2 comparisons and enlarge the target vocabulary; for listening training, however, it makes no sense.

Goal conflict

A fourth conflict results from diverging goals: teenagers watch movies for entertainment and relaxation, teachers use them to teach and want pupils to learn. "We must be careful to preserve the delicate balance between appreciating a film more because we understand the language, the culture, and the technique behind it, and killing the magic of the experience because we overdo the grammar, the vocabulary, or the pronunciation in the language and comprehension process" (Stempleski/Tomalin 2001: 9).

The final conflict stems from the fact that hardware and software equipment at schools as well as teachers' methodological know-how may lag behind technological requirements and standards.

Technology conflict

Conflicts in FBLL

Problems	*Solutions*
Time conflict: long film vs 45-minute lesson	• Time-saving forms of presentation • Independent film study
Language conflict: authentic material vs learners' level	• No "having-to-understand-everything-attitude" • Film selection adapted to learners' level • Simple plots • Slow, clear pronunciation (RP) • Repeated viewings • Pre-viewing activities • Few discrepancies between words and visuals
Reception conflict: visual vs auditory channel (subtitled films: "The eye is more powerful than the ear")	• Reflected combination of audio and subtitles • No exclusive use of subtitles • Tuning in (subtitles just for the first minutes)
Goal conflict: entertainment vs learning	• Balancing learning and enjoying • Restricted use of pause button • Avoiding over-analysis • Careful use of grammar / vocabulary exercises
Technology conflict: requirements vs school equipment / teacher know-how	• Pre-service training • In-service tutorials • Private notebook

1.12 Lesson Planning

Of course, there are manifold ways of integrating films into teaching English. A film may serve as a lead-in at the beginning, as an example to illustrate a certain point, as a goody to wrap up the lesson; it can also become the centre of one lesson or even a longer project. How a film is actually employed, depends, among others, on the teacher's objectives, the peculiarities of the film and the time available. If FBLL is pursued at a systematic level, training film-related competences must not be regarded as an

Variety of functions

isolated exercise, but should be organized within the framework of a well-structured lesson plan.

Traditional lesson pattern

For planning TEFL lessons, there are several models available (Thaler 2012: 9.2.), which can also be adapted to suit FBLL purposes. A traditional model used in some European trainee institutions (for 45-minute lessons) takes setting and checking (written and oral) homework into account and consists of the following stages:

A. Warming-up (ca. 2 minutes)
B. Discussing oral homework (ca. 6')
C. Checking written homework (ca. 7')
D. New content (ca. 28'): lead-in ➤ presentation ➤ securing comprehension ➤ practice ➤ use
E. Setting homework (ca. 2')

PWP

An even more widespread structural pattern is the PWP (pre – while – post) model, which is particularly suitable for training receptive competences such as reading, writing – and viewing. In the pre-viewing phase, the topic is introduced, background knowledge is activated, motivation is initiated. The while-viewing phase is supposed to facilitate understanding and check comprehension – beside short-term while-viewing, long-term while-viewing tasks, e. g. character development, should not be forgotten (Lütge 2012: 60). Analysis and follow-up work can finally be done in the post-viewing phase.

PPP

A third model, which also consists of three stages, is particularly recommended for beginners and the first contact with new language patterns: PPP: Presentation ➤ Practice ➤ Production.

TBLL

It is, however, opposed by supporters of Task-Based Language Learning (TBLL), who focus on communication, meaning and tasks, and therefore criticize PPP as being too rigid and formalistic. The most famous TBLL model has been devised by Jane Willis (1996), comprising three major stages as well as several sub-phases.

Pre-task
Introduction to topic and task

Task Cycle
Task — Planning — Report

Language Focus
Analysis — Practice

GTD

The global-to-detail approach is based on a double viewing of a film (scene) and progresses from a global to a detailed understanding of what has been presented: (1) introduction ➤ (2) First viewing ➤ (3) Global comprehension ➤ (4) Second viewing ➤ (5) Detailed comprehension ➤ (6) Follow-up.

10-step structure

Another lesson pattern, which refines the global-to-detail approach and has been designed particularly for promoting listening-viewing with shorter films, consists of ten phases.

10-Step Approach to Listening-Viewing

Step	*Phase*	*Functions*
1	Listening-viewing motivation	– Introducing the situation: Who? When? Where? – Justifying the need to watch
2	Preparatory work	– Pre-teaching key words / phrases – Explaining the (inter-)cultural background
3	First purpose	– Giving the intention, e.g. global understanding – Setting the tasks
4	First viewing	Presenting the whole film
5	Global comprehension	Presenting and discussing students' answers
6	Second purpose	– Giving the intention, e.g. detailed understanding – Setting the questions
7	Second viewing	Presenting the film a second time
8	Detailed comprehension	Presenting and discussing students' answers
9	(optional) Third viewing	– Presenting (a part or the whole) film a third time with a focusing task – Checking the answers
10	Wrap-up	Follow-up activities, analysis, discussion, transfer

Chronological lesson plan

Finally, chronological grids are often employed to give shape to the different dimensions of a lesson. The following plan offers six columns.

Time	Teacher	Learners	Interaction	Media	Objectives
2'	T greets L and talks about last night's movie	L participate in small talk	T-L talk	T, L	Warming-up
....	....	....	....	....	....

Orientation and variety

Far from offering perfect teaching recipes, these planning models should be understood as orientation guides, which do not have to be followed slavishly. Each of these models can and must be adapted depending on film genre, length, content, objectives, and viewing purpose. The more structural patterns one knows and tries out, however, the more freedom and confidence one gains, and the more varied one's lessons become. Variation is not only recommended for motivational reasons, but also to practise different types of viewing comprehension. Thus, even with the first viewing, it may be sensible to go for detailed comprehension, e. g. to watch out for some object in a commercial, or to identify a certain feeling in a person. Of course, separating the modes of perception is also possible, i.e. first only viewing or only listening, and then both – which may evoke stunning surprise effects.

Tasks

1. Name the five conflicts of FBLL. Choose one of them and point out how you would try to solve this conflict.
2. The film *Night on Earth* (1991), directed by Jim Jarmusch, is a collection of five short vignettes set during the same night in five cities. Watch the episode on the taxi drive in New York, in which a temporary bond is established between a black taxi driver and his passenger, who is acted by the wonderful Armin Müller-Stahl (http://www.youtube.com/watch?v=gdY24pZqAaw). Guided by the list of selection criteria, decide whether you can use it in a class of intermediate students (14-16 years).
3. If the answer to task 2 is "yes", design a 45-minute lesson plan for this episode.

2 Film Literacy

What should students in our classrooms aim to achieve when we show them films?

2.1 Model

Communication

Communicative Language Teaching (CLT), which stresses the interactive nature of communication and aims at communicative competence, has meanwhile become the dominant approach to teaching and learning a foreign language. In the field of intercultural learning, ICC (Intercultural Communicative Competence), which combines knowledge, skills and attitudes, is commonly regarded as the overall objective. Likewise, the ultimate goal of working with literature, i.e. LCC (Literary Communicative Competence), comprises the three domains of knowledge, skills and attitudes (e.g. Thaler 2012, 2008).

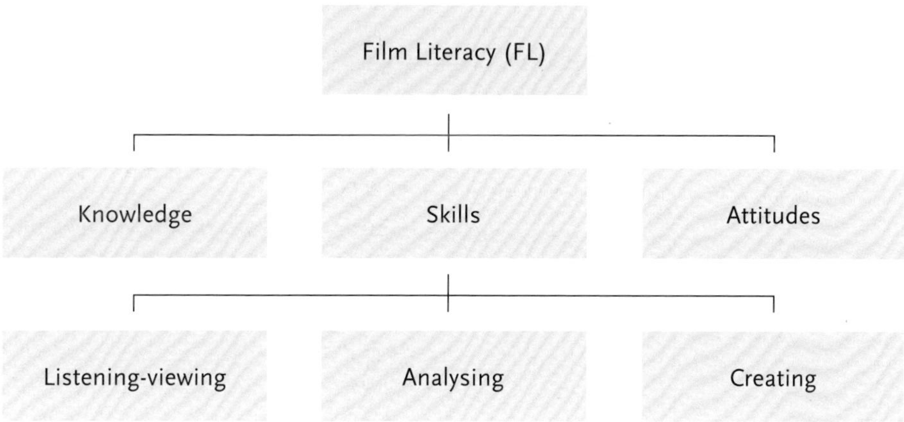

Film literacy

Drawing on those three models, the general aim of using audio-visual media in foreign language learning may be termed as *communicative film competence*, *audio-visual literacy*, or simply: *film literacy*. This concept also consists of three dimensions: knowledge, attitudes, and various skills, i.e. listening-viewing, analysing, and creating. The three domains as well as the three sub-skills must be seen against the background of foreign language communication. They should not be dealt with as separate dimensions, but foster film-based communication and negotiation of meaning (also see the two models of film literacy by Blell / Lütge, 2004: 404, and Lütge 2012: 25).

2.2 Knowledge

Relevance of knowledge

For primary and secondary schools, it would be exaggerated to demand some profound film knowledge from our students. A certain acquaintance with a selection of the most important issues, however, seems necessary – for students and teachers alike. If learners claim they do not need a theoretical background but want a 'direct', 'unbiased' approach to a film, they are not aware of their hidden theoretical premises. An insight into the theory, critique, and history of film helps them to discover their own subconscious guidelines of judgement. You are also less likely to 'misread' a film through ignorance of its theoretical concept or historical setting. Finally, the broader your information about the background of a film, the more multi-faceted, subtle, and fascinating it may become to you.

Film history

An overview of film history helps the viewers to orientate themselves, to ease their understanding of the details of a specific work, and to recognize intertextual references between various films. The following table only gives a rather rough survey of the history of film (Dixon / Foster 2008; www.filmsite.org/filmh.html). When teaching a certain film in class, it is recommended that teachers obtain specific information on it, e.g. from the Internet Movie Database (www.imdb.com).

A Short History of Film

Time	*Events*
late 19th century	Experiments in motion pictures: • Thomas Alva Edison' first movie machine, the *kinetoscope* (1891) • Louis and Auguste Lumiere's camera-projector, the *cinematographe* (1895)

1900 – 1920	• Edwin Porter: *The Great Train Robbery* (1903), 8 minutes, movies as mass entertainment • Silent films (accompanied by live musicians, intertitles) • Major studios in New York (shooting in 'dark' studios) • American filmmakers as pioneers • D.W. Griffith: most influential director, famous for his grammar of shots and lighting effects, *The Birth of a Nation* (1915): highly successful, film as art
1920 – 1940	• Shift of American filmmaking to Hollywood • Leading directors: DeMille, Lubitsch, Ford • variety of genres (epics, romantic comedies, westerns) • Charlie Chaplin: one of the first international movie stars (*The Kid*, 1921, *The Gold Rush*, 1925) • Sound movies: *The Jazz Singer* (1927) ➤ genres requiring witty or action-oriented dialogue (gangster movies, screwball comedies, extravagant musicals) • Climax of studio system (steady stream of films, stars): *Gone with the Wind* (1939)
1940s	• War and post-war dramas • Italian neorealism • British comedies and thrillers (*The Third Man*)
1950s	• Cold war era zeitgeist • Threat by TV, dwindling audiences, closure of cinemas and studios ➤ "bigger is better": Cinemascope (big screen), epic films (*Ben Hur*), gimmicks (3-D film) • Golden age of Asian cinema
1960s	• Decline of Hollywood studio system • Independent studios: high-quality original filmmaking • French nouvelle vogue, Italy's Fellini, Swedish Bergman • Hollywood: films reflecting social revolution
1970s	• New Hollywood, post-classical drama • Auteur style: Allen, Altman, Coppola, Scorsese • Adult cinemas (pornographic movies) • New German cinema (Herzog, Wenders, Fassbinder), Indian Bollywood, Australian film (*Picnic at Hanging Rock*)
1980s	• Videotape (VCR) • Blockbusters (Spielberg, Lucas) and sequels

1990s	• Special-effects films (*Titanic*) • Independent cinema in US • Danish Dogme 95 ➤ to purify filmmaking • Computer animation and digital cinema technology
2000 - 2013	• Documentary films (*Bowling for Columbine*) • Harry Potter film series • Increasing globalization of cinema • Revival in 3-D • *The Long Tail* (regular people write, shoot, and distribute their own films)

Film theory

Whereas film history is primarily concerned with historical areas of inquiry, film theory or film criticism deals with the systematic areas of film studies (e.g. Dyer 2000). It explores the narrative, artistic, cultural, social, economic, political and ideological implications of film and cinema.

Genre

One category in film theory which is of relevance for language classrooms, is *genre*. Of course, film classifications can never be precise, and many films are considered crossbreeds (hybrids) with several overlapping genre (or sub-genre) types. Yet, isolating certain elements in a film and categorizing them in genres, makes it possible to evaluate a film within its genre and to allow for comparisons and judgments on its value. The table below follows the basic distinction in genre between fiction and documentary, but only lists the most widespread genres of the first category (e.g. www.filmsite.org/genres.html). Thinking in terms of genre, however, should not lead to a neglect of the auteur system, in which films are rated with reference to one person, usually the director, because his / her style or vision determines the look and feel of the film, for example Woody Allen and comedy, Alfred Hitchcock and suspense, John Ford and westerns, or Errol Flynn and swashbuckler films.

Film Genres

Types	*Descriptions*
Action films	... usually include physical stunts and chases, often with scenes depicting rescues, fights, escapes, destructive crises (floods, explosions, fires, etc.), non-stop motion, and adventurous, often two-dimensional "good-guy" heroes battling "bad guys"' – primarily designed for pure audience escapism.

Adventure films	... usually follow exciting stories, often set in exotic locations, can include historical spectacles, traditional swashbucklers, serialized films, or treasure hunts.
Comedies	... have light-hearted plots deliberately designed to amuse and provoke laughter by exaggerating the situation, the language, action, relationships and characters; sub-types are slapstick, screwball, spoofs, romantic comedies, and black comedy.
Crime (gangster) films	... deal with the sinister actions of criminals, e.g. bankrobbers, underworld figures, or ruthless hoodlums who operate outside the law; they may be categorized as film noir or detective-mystery films.
Dramas	... display serious plots, portraying realistic characters, settings, and life situations; the stories often involve intense character development and interaction.
Epics	... take an historical or imagined event, a heroic figure, and add an extravagant setting and lavish costumes, accompanied by spectacle, dramatic scope, and a sweeping musical score; they include costume dramas, war films, medieval romps, or "period pictures" (covering a large expanse of time).
Fantasy films	... take the audience to netherworld transcending the bounds of human possibility and physical laws – unlike science fiction films that base their content upon some degree of scientific truth; they often have an element of magic, myth, wonder, escapism, and the extraordinary.
Horror films	... are designed to invoke our hidden worst fears, often in a terrifying finale, while captivating and entertaining us at the same time.
Musical / dance films	... are combinations of film narratives with music, dance, song or choreography.
Romance films	... are love stories, centring on passion and emotion, dominated by the affectionate involvement of the main characters (usually a man and a lady), and depicting the journey of their love through courtship or marriage.
Sci-fi films	... are visionary and quasi-scientific, packed with heroes, aliens, distant planets, fantastic settings, dark villains, and futuristic technology.
War (and anti-war) films	... acknowledge the horror of war, making the actual fighting on land, sea, or in the air the primary plot or background.
Westerns	... have easily recognizable plots, elements, and characters, e.g. cowboys, Indians, six-guns, horses, dusty towns and crowded saloons; as defining genre of the American film industry, they remind us of the early days of the expansive American frontier.

Film techniques

Apart from being informed about the (sub-) genres on the macro level of film studies, we need to know the tools on the micro level of classroom analysis. Cinematic techniques are the devices a director uses to communicate meaning and to arouse intended emotional responses in viewers (e. g. Konigsberg 1997, Surkamp 2010). That is why teachers and students have to learn form and (!) function of the most important techniques

(http://schools.dcsd.k12.nv.us/pwl/class/kerb/documents/l4_u2_activity2_15_se.pdf).

Cinematic Techniques	
Shots	
Shot	a single piece of film uninterrupted by cuts
Establishing shot	often a long shot ➤ to set the scene or show transitions between locations
Long shot (full shot)	a shot from some distance, e.g. showing the full body of a person ➤ may show the isolation or vulnerability of sb.
Medium shot	most common shot; camera seems to be a medium distance from the object / person ➤ to ground the story
Close up	image taking up at least 80 per cent of the frame ➤ to facilitate identification
Extreme close up	image being shot is a part of a whole, e. g an eye ➤ to focus on an object / emotion
Two shot	a scene shot exclusively from an angle that includes two characters equally ➤ love scenes
Camera angles	
Eye level	a shot taken from a normal height, i.e. the character's eye level ➤ most natural angle (90 % of the shots)
High angle	camera being above the subject ➤ to make the subject look smaller, weaker, powerless, trapped
Low angle	camera filming subject from below ➤ to make the subject look larger, stronger, powerful, threatening
Camera movements	
Pan	a stationary camera moving from side to side on a horizontal axis
Tilt	a stationary camera moving up or down along a vertical axis

Zoom	a stationary camera with the lens moving ➤ to make an object seem to move closer to or further away from the camera ➤ moving into a character: revealing movement; moving away: distancing the audience from the character
Dolly / Tracking	the camera being on a track ➤ to move with the action
	Lighting
High key	the scene being flooded with light ➤ to create a bright and open looking scene
Low key	the scene being flooded with shadows and darkness ➤ to create suspense or suspicion
Bottom or side lighting	direct lighting from below or the side ➤ to make the subject appear dangerous or evil
Front or back lighting	soft lighting on the actor's face or from behind ➤ to give the appearance of innocence or goodness
	Editing
Cut	most common editing technique: two pieces of film are spliced together to "cut" to another image
Fade	to or from black or white: beginning in darkness and gradually assuming brightness (fade-in), or image gradually getting darker (fade-out) ➤ to imply that time has passed; to signify the end of a scene
Dissolve	kind of fade with one image being slowly replaced by another ➤ to create a connection between images
Wipe	a new image wiping off the previous one ➤ more fluid than a cut and quicker than a dissolve
Flashback	cutting or dissolving to action that happened in the past ➤ to show events in the past; to explain present behaviour
Cross cutting (parallel editing)	cutting into action that is happening simultaneously ➤ to create tension; to form a connection between scenes
	Sound
Diegetic	sound that could be heard by the characters in the film ➤ to heighten authenticity
Non-diegetic	sound that cannot be heard by the characters ➤ to trigger audience reaction (e.g. ominous music for foreshadowing)

2.3 Skills

Three main skills

As films constitute a central medium of cultural representation, it is essential to learn to "read" films, i.e. to understand their contents and analyse forms and functions of different formats (Monaco 2009). Viewing a film is not synonymous with understanding it. If you examine it more closely, you can ultimately reach a deeper appreciation of it. Analysis, i.e. studying the individual components of a film, and interpretation, i.e. exploring the potential meanings of it, may go hand in hand during this process. Apart from listening-viewing and analyzing a film, learners should also be encouraged to personally relate to a text on a creative level.

Thus there are three basic skills to be promoted in FBLL:

- Listening-viewing
- Analyzing
- Creating

Interdependence

These three skills, however, should not be considered as separate skills practised in isolation. They are interdependent, overlap each other and can be linked in the different stages of a teaching unit.

Importance of listening-viewing

The relevance of listening-viewing and the necessity of its systematic training in foreign language classrooms are by now beyond doubt: The ratio between spoken and written language in everyday communication is 95 % : 5 %, audio-visual elements have become omnipresent in professional, educational and leisure domains (*visual turn, audio-visual era*), listening and viewing are preconditions for other language activities (listening comes before speaking), and related studies on listening comprehension suggest that classes with a targeted audio-visual instruction perform better than their control groups – even in other linguistic areas (e.g. Anderson / Lynch 1995, Kieweg et al. 2003).

Separate competence

Due to these findings, educational standards and school curricula have integrated listening-viewing in their lists of competences. Although it is usually classified as a variant of listening, it must be regarded as a separate competence in its own right, which is far more complex than listening: Learners simultaneously receive an auditory and a visual input, the process of listening comprehension must be synchronized with the one of viewing comprehension, i.e. spoken texts have to be understood, images to be interpreted, para-linguistic features to be decoded, and to be put into a logical relationship. If textual elements (e. g. subtitles, inserts) are added, listening-viewing is even expanded to listening-viewing-reading.

Listening-viewing model

In analogy to the listening process, listening-viewing unfolds in some interactive relation between bottom-up and top-down processes. The different components of listening-viewing competence are summarized in the table below (Thaler 2012: 170).

Listening-Viewing	
Listening	Viewing
• general competence (e. g. knowledge of the world) • linguistic competence (e. g. ability to discriminate sounds) • prosodic competence (e. g. ability to interpret intonation and pitch) • socio-pragmatic competence (e. g. ability to identify text types) • strategic competence (e. g. ability to apply culture-specific scripts / schemata)	• understanding actions • interpreting iconic elements (images, scenery, objects) • interpreting paralingual features (gestures, mime, posture, eye contact, distance) • understanding cinematographic techniques (colours, light, camera angles, cuts) • knowledge of the world, intercultural knowledge • reading comprehension (subtitles, inserts, written texts in the picture)

▼

Relationship between sound and image
• time: at the same time or one after the other • content: congruence or contradiction • processing: perception, storage and comparison of sound and image

Pre-viewing stage

When promoting listening-viewing in language classes, teachers may structure their lessons according to the PWP approach (pre – while – post viewing). In the pre-viewing stage, they may start with some of the following activities (Thaler 2012: 174).

Pre-Viewing Activities	
Upside down comprehension	Students answer questions on the film before (!) watching it, and check their answers after watching.
Associations	Students collect associations on the title or the topic of the film (brainstorming, heartstorming, mind mapping).
Predicting the opening scene	Students speculate about the opening scene on the basis of DVD cover, poster or advertisements.
Listening to the soundtrack	Students listen to the theme music and speculate about the content of the film.

While-viewing stage

In the while-viewing stage, it is, first of all important that the film is understood. Teachers have to decide which type of understanding is to be expected from the learners. Some vague assignment like "listen and watch" is likely to provoke the unrealistic intention of wanting to understand every single word. To avoid such excessive demands including the frustration resulting from them, the intention has to be specified. The following categories can be distinguished:

- Global comprehension ➤ communicative situation, topic
- Selective comprehension ➤ certain facts
- Detailed comprehension ➤ details

As a rule, films are exploited by several, if not all of these types of comprehension – which makes it even more important to clearly tell the class before each viewing, which of these forms is expected from them.

Closed activities …

As to the activities in the while-viewing stage, one should vary between open, semi-open, and closed formats (also see Einhoff 2011). Closed activities comprise:

- multiple choice
- true / false (not in the text)
- matching: e. g. characters and statements, texts and headings, text passages and pictures, halves of sentences
- putting jumbled sentences / passages into the right order
- ordering jumbled pictures
- identifying differences between listening text and transcript
- spotting errors in the script
- identifying *mondegreens* (mishearings)
- choosing between alternatives (e. g. two words given)

Closed formats are more valid than answers to questions, for example, as they only check listening-viewing comprehension, but not writing skills. The reduced amount of language output may lead to a guilty conscience creeping over some teachers, but closed formats are necessary for tests which are supposed to be objective, valid, reliable – and economic. For the sake of methodological variety, progression of requirements, and classroom atmosphere, more open and complex activities should also be applied though. Therefore the following overview of while-viewing tasks particularly mentions such open formats (Thaler 2012: 175).

... and open activities

Open While-Viewing Activities	
Blind listening	Students listen to sound, music and dialogue only; then they speculate about the film.
Silent viewing	Students watch the film without sound and imagine what the characters are saying, what may be happening.
Split viewing	Half of the students watch without listening, the others listen without watching; then they try to reconstruct the film together.
Going beyond the limits	Students watch an excerpt of the film and imagine what happened before and how the plot will develop.
Fast forward / rewind	Students summarize the plot after watching the film with fast forward or rewind.
Jumbled sequence	Different scenes are shown in the wrong order; students try to find the right order.
Class chain	One after the other, students give an oral summary of a film, each contributing only one sentence.
Choosing a summary	Students each write a summary; then they vote on the best.
Lie detector test	The teacher summarizes a film and inserts some errors. Students shout "lie!" when they find a mistake and correct it.
Question pot	Students draw a slip of paper from a pot and answer the question on it after watching the film.
Task dice	Students throw the dice and do the task connected to their number, e. g. summary, description (of a setting or person), pantomime, drawing, quote etc.
Film dice	Students throw a dice with general beginnings of sentences (I liked ..., I disliked ..., I didn't understand ..., It surprised me ..., The best thing ..., The strangest thing ...) and use them to comment on the film.

Open While-Viewing Activities	
Film domino	One student writes a key word about the film on the blackboard, the others continue, starting with the last letter of the key word (e. g. love – eternal – lie ...).
My favourite scene	Students describe setting, characters und plot in their favourite scene.
Ticket vote	After watching a movie, students throw their tickets in one of three boxes (good – satisfactory – bad) and discuss the results.
Freeze frame	Students describe a film still.
Asking the director	Students watch an excerpt and write down 'why' questions for the director. When they watch for the second time, they also listen to the voice-over commentary and try to find his answers.
Film response journal	Students enter their observations on a film they watched outside the classroom in a journal – possibly guided by w-questions.

DVDs

Modern DVDs come along with various bonus materials, which can appropriately be integrated into the while-viewing stage (e. g. interviews with directors / actors or deleted scenes). In particular, the subtitles offer various options for classroom activities. With difficult films or passages, English subtitles can be switched on to facilitate listening comprehension. Subtitles do serve as an aid to understanding, yet they can also overload the pupils with additional reading and may distract attention away from the visuals. If you want to discuss subtitling procedures in more detail, you can compare them with the spoken text. Mother tongue subtitles as a comprehension aid should be avoided, as learners are overstrained when they have to decode visuals, English listening text and L1 reading text at the same time – with the consequence that they only focus on the German text. L1 subtitles, however, lend themselves to a contrastive analysis of idiomatic expressions, or a comparison with the subtitles written by the learners themselves.

Transcripts

A further way of working on the textual code is provided by transcripts, which are now available on several websites (e. g. www.imdb.com). They can be applied, above all, to language training, especially in promoting listening comprehension, but also in checking listening-viewing comprehension (see the last two ideas in the following table).

Working with the Transcript	
Complete text with changes	*Incomplete text*
• putting sentences / passages in the correct order • finding discrepancies between transcript and film • choosing between alternative words • identifying words that are not in the film • replacing symbols with words	• filling gaps • completing words in a C-Test (the second half of each second word is missing) • filling in specific types of words (e. g. all adjectives) • matching the two halves of a sentence • matching text passages and film stills • matching quotes and characters

Analysing

The while-reading stage is also the place for film analysis (e. g. Sherman 2001, Stempleski / Tomalin 2003, Boggs / Petrie 2008, Monaco 2009, Grünewald 2009, Lütge 2012, Dasenbrock / Lütge 2013). The specific devices of film-making and the combination of image and sound can be studied during this phase in more or less detail. When teachers want to analyse (parts of) a film, they should draw learners' attention to the specific elements of this medium and their effects in the three constituent dimensions, i.e. the cinematic dimension, the dramatic dimension, and the literary dimension.

Film Analysis	
Dimensions	*Aspects*
Cinematic dimension	• camera movement • camera angles • camera speed • field sizes • editing, montage • sound, music • colour, lighting
Dramatic dimension	• casting • acting • dialogues • locations • props • make-up • costumes

Film Analysis	
Dimensions	*Aspects*
Literary dimension	• story • topics • characters • setting • narrative point of view

Analysis activities

The foundations of film analysis should already be laid in lower classes, and refined in later years (e. g. Surkamp 2010). It can be supported by worksheets with illustrations of the various cinematic devices (Dasenbrock / Lütge 2013: very useful copies), and various types of observation sheets, viewing grids, note-taking sheets (Teasley / Wilder 1997, Lütge 2012: 34ff.). As well as comprehension and analysis questions, they may include true / false statements, gapped texts, matching exercises, or spot the lie texts. However, it is vital that learners are not forced to document every camera angle and editing technique in each scene, making them believe that film literacy is synonymous with having an abundant film glossary at one's permanent disposal. Similar to working with literary texts, observations need to be linked to intended effects in order to analyse the functions of cinematic devices. If possible, learners should be able to experience the various effects, e. g. when a scene (without any text) is presented with different soundtracks, and the changes in atmosphere are compared. Additionally they may even be stimulated to reflect on parallels between formal techniques and their own personal lives, e. g. when discussing Charlie Chaplin's aphorism: "Life is a tragedy when seen in close-up, but a comedy in long-shot."

Post-viewing stage

The post-viewing stage focuses on transcending comprehension, i.e. mental activities going beyond the text itself such as inferencing, elaborating, extracting, generalizing, evaluating, commenting, constructing, and creating. The following list contains a few suggestions for corresponding tasks.

Post-Viewing Tasks	
Press conference	Students do a role play: a press conference with actors and journalists.
Debate	A controversial topic from the film is discussed in a formal debate.
Review	Students write a film review (and publish it on the Internet).
Film projects	Students work on different film-related projects, e. g. film guide, movie magazine, trailer, script, etc.
Open ending	Students imagine the continuation of the plot for a film with an open ending.
Famous last words	The very last frame of the film is frozen and students imagine the last words spoken.
Wishing you were here	Students summarize the plot from the point of view of one character in the film.
The story within the story	Students tell the life story of a minor character in the film.
Moving the goal posts	Students imagine how the plot might have developed with different characters, at a different time, in a different place.
Making comparisons	Students compare film and novel, two reviews / trailers of the same film.

The post-viewing stage is also a particularly good place for practicing creative skills. Individually, in pairs or small groups, learners may present their personal perspectives on a film. Creativity need not be confined to the written mode, but can include spoken, manual, scenic, acoustic, visual, and, of course, audio-visual forms.

Creating

Creating	
Medium	*Examples*
Written creations	• writing a script for a scene • writing on the title (pre-viewing phase)
Spoken creations	• speaking a dialogue over a silent viewing scene • discussing the quality of the film in a flash debate
Manual creations	• designing a film poster • producing a film collage
Scenic creations	• role playing a dialogue • parodying the Oscars award ceremony

Creating	
Medium	*Examples*
Acoustic creations	• choosing suitable soundtracks • making appropriate noises
Visual creations	• drawing a structure chart • making a film magazine
Audio-visual creations	producing a film

Film production

Producing one's own film may be regarded as the logical climax of film literacy. Web-based tools enable even beginners to become movie producers. Websites like www.digitalfilms.com, for example, ask us to unleash our creativity by making our digital film online for free. All we have to do is to choose a background scene, characters, animated actions, dialogue, introduction, and ending credits; after five minutes, we can put our name as the producer and email the movie to our friends or teachers.

Film production extended

Of course, you get more options when producing your movie with your own recording devices (Thaler 1999, 2008, Henseler / Möller / Surkamp 2011: 141ff.). Due to technological progress, anybody can advance to become a film producer these days, without too much effort and special know-how. With the help of a cellphone, camcorder or webcam you can shoot short clips, which may then be uploaded at video sharing websites like YouTube – or even sent to foreign language competitions, e. g. *Bundeswettbewerb Fremdsprachen*. Those who want to integrate Web 2.0 in their classrooms, may be guided by the following 10 learning levels ranging from sampling to sharing (Thaler 2008). The diagram below shows this framework, which allows for individual and flexible use as teachers do not have to go through all the various stages, but may select those that suit their interests and objectives best.

10-level pyramid

Sampling, i.e. watching several videos at video sharing websites on a certain topic or genre, constitutes the first step (1). The rather passive task of sampling should be supplemented by comprehension tasks (2): the understanding of the content is checked, the language used in the videos is practised (competences, skills, grammar, vocabulary). Then the video is analysed (3) by drawing the learners' attention to aspects like source, authorship, technical quality, cinematic devices, message, impact, socio-cultural background (Fraser / Oram 2004, Stempleski / Tomalin 2001). The objective analysis of the video should then be elaborated on by a personal

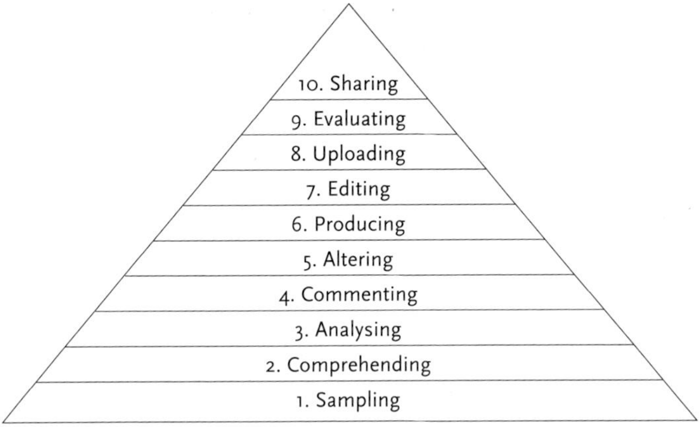

comment (4). As most video sharing websites have a 'comment' button, students can express their own opinion in written form online. With the help of a subtitle editor (e. g. White Horse), students may add subtitles or captions (5). The next step of producing one's own video (6) constitutes the central stage of the learning process as the development of film literacy is linked to learners gaining experience by taking an active role. The video can be produced with the help of a digital camera, camcorder or just a mobile phone. Experience has shown that preparing and producing the video are facilitated by a storyboard, which may look like this:

Storyboard

Project title: ....

Take No.	Action	Dialogue	Setting, camera, sound, props etc.
1			
2			
3			
....			

Then the video can be edited (7), i.e. it is cut, a title is added, music and effects are selected, which may be done with the help of a simple tool like Movie Maker. After a user account at a video sharing website has been opened, uploading (8) the video from the PC (or mobile, camera, camcorder) just takes a few seconds. Evaluating (9) should cover three areas, i.e. assessing the product (video), the process (project work) and the discourse (social relevance of video sharing websites). The final step is sharing (10) with regard to showing the video to other people and encouraging them to participate in this kind of communication (at a video sharing website).

p decalogue

Adopting such a creative approach to FBLL conforms to the *p decalogue of media literacy* (Thaler 2012):

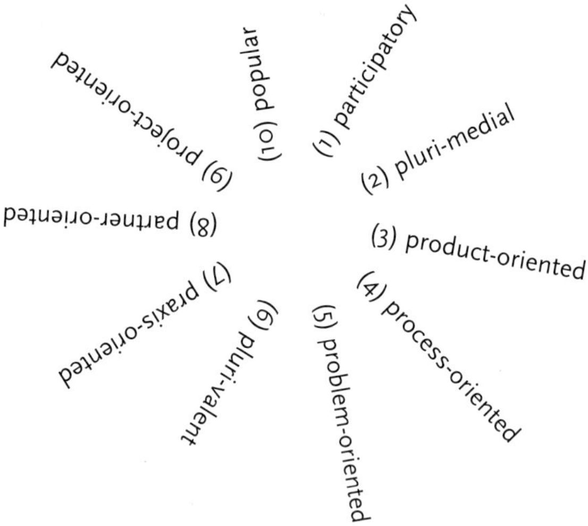

2.4 Attitudes

Enjoyment

Viewing for information is one goal, viewing for enjoyment may be another aim in language classes. Whether you want to follow an exciting plot, share the hero's / heroine's experiences, learn from how they deal with psychological or moral problems, get to know different approaches to life, study a director's cinematic skills, become enthralled by an actor's performance, or be led to a deeper understanding of yourselves – films can provide pleasure and enjoyment. Thus a film can sometimes be watched simply for its own sake – using language products like normal consumers, and cherishing them. "The camera's eye can capture the grimmest realities and also conjure up the most lavish and extravagant fantasies; it can bring us closer to the world and provide a welcome escape from its rigors. Above all, cinema is a means of communication, a medium through which the range of human experience – the difficult emotions, the piquant absurdities, the heroic possibilities – is shared and expanded" (Scott 2004).

Sense of quality

Teachers may also want to help pupils judge the quality of a film. It is true that aesthetic judgements are problematic as there is no generally accepted canon of criteria, and *de gustibus non est disputandum*. But if we try to develop in our learners the ability to look critically at the quality of films, they can make better decisions as to which film to watch, and they are likely to appreciate those films at a deeper level. They may not only be able to identify means of cheap entertainment like vulgarity, obscenity, or violence, but also recognize the numerous shades between beautiful and ugly, humorous and tragic, sublime and hilarious, fascinating and boring, authentic and pretentious, real and fake.

Intercultural learning

Watching films can also contribute to intercultural learning (e. g. Hescher 2009, Küchler 2009, Schumann 2009). When our students view a foreign movie, they experience other value systems and are encouraged to compare home and foreign identities, which fosters critical cultural awareness. Teaching foreign films can encourage the breaking down of barriers, ask the viewers to decentre from their own positions, make them reflect on auto- and hetero-stereotypes, all of which can lead to a better understanding between various cultures. As a *moving picture book*, video gives access to things, places, people, events and behaviour, and so films help to substitute for the experience of living in an English-speaking country (Sherman 2003).

Media education

Finally, a major goal in working with audio-visual materials is media education. Learners should be able to understand and look critically at the nature, techniques and impacts of film messages and productions. By discovering the suggestive power of media and reflecting it, they learn to stand back and avoid purely passive consumption. For example, they have to become aware of these aspects:

- Films are constructions: They are created with a certain purpose, adopting a particular perspective, using specific techniques, conveying ideological messages, transporting notions of values, power and beauty.

- Films are commercial products: Media production is a business and must make a profit.
- Films are read by us: Audiences negotiate meaning, and each of us makes sense of what he / she sees / hears in different ways.

Open process

Film education is not primarily about having the right answers, but rather about asking the right questions. As film issues are complex and controversial, teachers should not only be able to impart knowledge, but also facilitate the process of dialogue, interaction and communication.

Tasks

1. Cinematic techniques: The following text summarizes field sizes, camera movements, camera positions and camera angles, including their general effects. Fill in the gapped text with the following cinematic terms (Thaler 2008):
   bird's eye view – crane shot – establishing shot – extreme close-up – eye-level shot – medium – over-the-shoulder shot – panning – point-of-view shot – shot – static shot – tilting – tracking shot – worm's eye view – zooming
2. How can you work with the clip *Do you speak English* in a TEFL classroom? In this hilarious short comedy by Simon Pegg and the Big Train comedy sketch team, an English speaking tourist whose car has broken down in France attempts to speak to two locals in different languages, but they obstinately pretend to not understand her. (www.youtube.com/watch?v=fijBUeqiWog)
3. Are you going to produce a film with the students in your English language class? State your opinion.

Film Techniques

Field size refers to the kind and size of shot in a film. A long .... (a) shows people and objects from a distance, giving a complete view of the setting. The whole body or object is presented in a full shot. A .... (b) shot zooms in closer on the actors and shows the upper body or part of an object. Head and shoulders are usually seen in a close-up, which draws the attention to the face, e.g. in order to show emotions. To focus the most important object or part of a face in a scene, a detailed shot or .... (c) is employed.
The simplest form of *camera movement* is the .... (d), when the camera does not move, which evokes a calm and peaceful state. .... (e) means the camera moves from left to right or vice versa, which may give the viewer a feeling of orientation. The camera going up and down is called .... (f), which often increases tension by examining something in greater detail. In a .... (g) the camera is placed on a vehicle moving on the ground. When the camera moves flexibly in all directions high up on a crane, we speak of a .... (h). .... in can focus important details, zooming out discloses the whole context of the situation.
Camera positions comprise, among others, a .... (j), which shows the action through a character's eyes, an .... (k), which shows the location at the start of a scene, and an .... (l), emphasizing the role of the speaker or listener in a dialogue.
Of the three basic *camera angles*, an .... (m) is neutral and undramatic, whereas a high-angle shot (from above), also called .... (n), makes people seem smaller, weak and inferior, and the low-angle shot (from below), also called .... (o), makes people seem bigger, powerful, superior or threatening.

Short Formats

3 Music Videos

- Have you ever watched a music video in English lessons?
- Is there anything useful music videos may teach our students?
- Can music videos make a contribution to our students' film literacy?

3.1 Theory

Definition

A music video is a short film combining a song and visuals, thus consisting of three components: music, lyrics and video (Thaler 1999). The visual code may not only be used to illustrate or emphasize the other two layers, but can also contradict them or show only little relation to them. The clip usually lasts as long as the original song, occasionally it comes along with pre- or / and post-sequences. A rather long pre-sequence can be observed in Lady Gaga's *Marry the Night*, whereas *Everybody* by The Backstreet Boys exemplifies a shorter pre- and post-sequence.

Functions

Music videos are produced for promotional or artistic purposes (*ad vs art*), they "must fulfill competing demands of showcasting the star, reflecting the lyrics, and underscoring the music" (Vernallis 2004: 4). The primary function is definitely to promote the single as well as the whole album by the artist(s) for the sake of maximum sales – "the message is BUY". Moreover, music videos are vital in constructing and promoting the image of a singer or a band on the way to stardom. They can also be a marketing product for other media, e.g. films (Fraser 2005: 8).

Types

Music videos display an enormous number of varieties in style – in varying quality (*trash or treasure*). There are recordings of a concert, narrative performances, animated short movies, abstract art videos, etc. The most general way to classify them is to divide them into *performance videos* and *concept videos*. The first focus on the musicians playing the song on stage, in studio or other settings; here the lip-synching musician is the centre of attention. The latter show different aspects of the lyrics illustrated with pictures or short film fragments (associative concept video), or the song is transformed into a coherent story (narrative concept video). Two special types are *typo clips* and *literal music videos*. A *typo clip* (*lyrics video*) makes the words of a song constitute the main element of the video, using lettering to an amazing effect and allowing lyrics to come to life. Two famous examples are *Sign o' the Times* by Prince (1987), which features the words of the song pulsing to the music, accompanied by abstract geometric shapes, and *Praying For Time* by George Michael (1990), who refused to make a traditional music video, releasing a clip that displayed the lyrics on a black screen (for more examples see: www.creativebloq.com/typography/typography-music-videos-11121409). A really humorous and didactically gainful variant is the *literal music video*, which is a parody of a music video with the original lyrics being replaced by lyrics that describe the visuals in the video (Thaler 2010).

Cinematic devices

The most common form of editing music videos is fast-cut montage, i.e. the images are cut at a very high frequency, often in harmony with the rhythm of the song, making it very hard for the viewers to identify them prima facie. Another major device is camera work, which emphasises the rhythm of the song and movements of the musicians. The clips also contain a lot of close-up shots to intensify the feeling of intimacy between the artist and the viewer. A lot of videos come with fast moving dance scenes and lavish choreography – just remember the king of pop, Michael Jackson, and his dance sequences in *Thriller* or *Bad* – but contemporary R&B singers like Usher or Beyoncé often seem to be astonishing dancers as well. Music videos also display an opulent metaphorical imagery, e. g. lots of symbols, allusions, intertextual and intermedial references. A famous video referring to a movie classic (*Metropolis*) is *Radio Ga-Ga* by Queen, another is Red Hot Chili Peppers' *Californication*, which is animated like an adventure video game (Fraser 2005: 30, Henseler / Möller / Surkamp 2011: 180).

History

Music videos represent a fusion of modern mass entertainment (film, TV, rock music) and artistic avantgarde (abstract film, video art, performance art). When music was no longer only played on the radio, but also on television, the music industry hit on the idea of producing a clipping of pictures you can broadcast over and over again (Sibilla 2010: 225). The origins of music videos date back much further (at least to Oskar Fischinger's animated commercials in the 1930s, maybe even back to stone age cave paintings), but they took centre stage in the 1980s, when MTV based its format around the new medium (Thaler 1999,

Keazor / Wübbena 2007). In 1981, the U.S. video channel Music Television launched *Video Killed the Radio Star*, a title as martial as it is programmatic, beginning an era of 24-hour-a-day music on television. With this new outlet for popular music, the music video quickly grew to play a central role in music marketing, supported by two key innovations in technology, i.e. relatively inexpensive and easy-to-use video recording and editing equipment, and the development of visual effects. In those days a lot of directors, who later became influential movie directors, started their careers by experimenting with music videos, e. g. David Fincher, famous for popular movies (*The Curious Case of Benjamin Button*, *Seven*, *Fight Club*), directed music videos for Sting, Madonna and Aerosmith. In the 90s, music video production costs were ever-increasing, with *Scream* by Janet and Michael Jackson becoming the most expensive one ever costing 7 million dollars in 1995.

Current developments

Today music channels like MTV do not broadcast video clips all day long anymore, but they have integrated reality shows, soap operas and animated cartoons into their daily programme. When music videos are presented, their length is often reduced, and there is at least one advertising banner at the bottom or the top of the screen covering parts of the video.

Today people also watch music clips on video sharing websites like "youtube.com". Yet, due to legal issues, the original video clips of the latest hits are often not available on those platforms as the society for musical copyright enforcement (e. g. GEMA) blocks many such videos. Although there are still a few famous artists who take pride in producing extravagant music videos for their hits, for example Lady Gaga or Madonna (Henseler / Möller / Surkamp 2011: 178), on average production budgets have been reduced resulting in a great number of rather simply produced videos, which only show the band performing live on stage. The movement towards using "low-fi"-aesthetics, i.e. clips which have the look of user generated internet videos, is strengthened by the era of Web 2.0, allowing everybody to make a music video at home and upload it to the web (Sibilla 2010: 230). If the video version of a hit is not available, users often lend a helping hand by creating their DIY versions of it. Newcomer bands see advantages when distributing their music via video to the internet users, because the web reaches people more directly and all over the world. Post-modernist ideology also favours making a mashup, i.e. a new arrangement of scenes of two or more original video clips, even mixing up several artists from different genres – just look at exciting examples like Queen vs. Daft Punk with *Another One Bites the Funk* (www.youtube.com/watch?v=Au16TTI7nQc), or AC / DC vs. 2Pac with *California Jazz* (www.youtube.com/watch?v=nvgVo2Suq-A).

Future

"In ten years' time straight promo channels like MTV will have ceased to be": That is what Simon Frith, professor of film and media studies, categorically stated in 1988 (!) (Thaler 2005: 23) – in 2014 they are still not extinct. There are also indicators that music videos will not vanish in the near future. Televisions are being replaced by hybrid TVs with internet connection, and digital cameras as well as smartphones can record a movie in HD quality. There is plenty of affordable video editing software (e. g. iMovie) available, which allows amateurs to produce a hiqh quality video. Nearly every pupil owns a smartphone with web access, on which they watch music videos and share them with their friends. Interactivity will also increase, for instance, making it possible to perform a virtual dance with your idol in a 3D music video game. The new technology of organic LEDs will allow the building of a video screen on every surface, including T-shirts or wallpaint (Wetzel / Jegl 2010: 263-265).

Rationale

Thus, also in the future, TEFL will be able to make use of music videos. It combines the advantages of teaching with pop songs and teaching with films. Visualisations of current pop songs can especially catch pupils' attention and are welcome as an authentic change from the daily textbook routine (Thaler 2012: 65-68). They can motivate students, because they are popular media formats, which they also watch in their spare-time. Moreover, seeing and listening to a music video is an experience for the class that might spark opportunities for speaking, writing, creative work, cinematic analysis, and can lead students from passive hearing to conscious and reflective listening (Lütge 2012: 7f.). Music videos also promote the intercultural competences of students: Cultural differences between C1 and C2, e. g. celebrating Christmas (UK: crackers, mistletoe, pumpkin pie, singing Christmas carols), can be illustrated by watching a video like *Rockin around the Christmas Tree* by Mel Smith and Kim Wilde (Thaler 2012: 277). Some music videos (Michael Jackson's *Black or White*, *American Skin (41 Shots)* by Bruce Springsteen) may also sharpen students' awareness of intercultural problems, e. g. racism, ethnical discrimination and xenophobia. Teaching English with music videos can indeed be a highly enjoyable and didactically rewarding experience for students – and teachers (Fraser 2005: 9).

3.2 Methodology

Sources

On the one hand, there are countless DVDs, Blue Rays or even videocassettes of artists on the market, which can be rented or bought. On the other, the number one source for music videos now is the internet, and web pages like youtube.com or myvideo.de provide countless music videos legally and often for free. The following list suggests some useful links (also see Henseler / Möller / Surkamp 2011: 184).

Music Video Sources	
Learning English via music videos	• http://www.multimedia-english.com/contenidos/channel/music/9 (music videos plus transcript of lyrics, word annotations, summaries, interpretation, background information, difficulty, accent, rating)
Music video channels	• www.youtube.com • www.clipfish.de • www.myvideo.de • www.tape.tv
Music video databases	• www.popzoot.tv/cliparchiv
Music video magazines	• www.popzoot.tv
Music television channels (with charts)	• www.mtv.com • www.vh1.com • www.viva.tv
Literal music videos	• www.huffingtonpost.com/2009/08/03/the-7-best-literal-music_n_249976.html
Songs inspired by literature (SIBL)	• www.youtube.com/watch?v=FdRVPzonNTA • www.siblproject.org
Karaoke channels	• www.youtube.com/user/TheKARAOKEChannel • www.karaoke-videos.net • www.dailymotion.com/hub/xvx_karaoke
Lyrics collections	• www.azlyrics.com • www.lyrics.com

Selection

As there is so much music on the market, teachers may feel spoilt for choice and should first get an overview of what their learners are actually listening to. It is certainly possible to use classics from Michael Jackson or R.E.M., yet learners may also resent *oldies but goldies*, as they seem old-fashioned, not up to the current technical standard and visual language, and strange for students' viewing habits. If you resort to current videos, the chances are higher that your students already know the performer, the video and the issues raised in it, which facilitates understanding. So it is recommended that you get in touch with the music of the day by checking the current charts. mtv.com is especially helpful because, besides studying the charts you can pick video premieres or popular videos chosen by viewers as well as MTV staff, and browse through various playlists of popular videos (Fisher 2013). You can also get your students involved in the process of choosing a video, but you have to make sure that the language and content of it is appropriate for school use.

A way of combining student autonomy and teacher guidance would be to have the pupils select the video, with the teacher then designing a lesson on it. Even if at first sight a video does not seem to be appropriate, you can adapt it for your students' level by choosing a suitable approach – for example, Michael Jackson's Earth Song has been used both for beginners and advanced learners (Thaler 1999).

Criteria

Further criteria of selection should be the following (Thaler 2002: 7):

- didactic efficiency (aims, topics, methods)
- link to reality (current events, seasons, anniversaries)
- difficulty (acoustic comprehensibility, lexical-structural progression, semantics)
- musical factors (sound volume, tune, refrain)
- genre (only narrative clips or performance and concept videos as well?)
- artistic quality (only aesthetically good clips or learning from the negative?)
- pedagogical suitability (violence, sexuality, sexism, banality?)
- availability

Thematic clipography

If you are looking for a video on a certain topic you have to deal with in class, the following survey on selected (classical) clips may help you.

Clipography

Topic	*Artists*	*Title*
Politics	Genesis Billy Joel Sting USA For Africa	LAND OF CONFUSION LENINGRAD RUSSIANS WE ARE THE WORLD
Irish Question	Cranberries Simple Minds U 2	ZOMBIE BELFAST CHILD SUNDAY BLOODY SUNDAY
War & Peace	Paul Hardcastle Passengers Bruce Springsteen	19 – THE FINAL STORY MISS SARAJEVO BORN IN THE USA
Social Problems	Phil Collins Madonna Bobby McFerrin Soul Asylum	ANOTHER DAY IN PARADISE MATERIAL GIRL DON'T WORRY BE HAPPY RUNAWAY TRAIN
Minorities & Racism	Tracy Chapman Eddie Grant Ice T UA Against Apartheid	ACROSS THE LINES GIMME HOPE JO'ANNA I MUST STAND SUN CITY
Growing Up & School	Boomtown Rats Coolio Crash Test Dummies Pearl Jam Pink Floyd	I DON'T LIKE MONDAYS GANGSTA'S PARADISE MMM MMM MMM MMM JEREMY ANOTHER BRICK IN THE WALL
Environment	Michael Jackson Pink Floyd R.E.M.	EARTH SONG TAKE IT BACK EVERYBODY HURTS

City	Jimi Hendrix Michael Jackson Pet Shop Boys	CROSSTOWN TRAFFIC BEAT IT SUBURBIA
Future & Space	Michael Jackson Police	SCREAM WALKING ON THE MOON
Religion	Genesis Madonna	JESUS HE LOVES YOU LIKE A PRAYER
Media	The Buggles U 2	VIDEO KILLED THE RADIO STAR BETTER THAN THE REAL THING
World of Pop Music	Dire Straits Tom Petty	MONEY FOR NOTHING INTO THE GREAT WIDE OPEN
Love & Friendship	Cave & Minogue Dire Straits	WHERE THE WILD ROSES GROW ROMEO & JULIET
Homosexuality & AIDS	Neneh Cherry Holly Johnson	I'VE GOT YOU UNDER MY SKIN LEGENDARY CHILDREN
Horror	Michael Jackson Metallica	THRILLER ENTER SANDMAN
Christmas	Bing Crosby Frankie Goes To Hollywood Wham	WHITE CHRISTMAS THE POWER OF LOVE LAST CHRISTMAS

Pre-viewing questionnaire

A good way to get in touch with your pupils' music tastes and attitudes towards music videos is to hand out the following questionnaire, have it analysed by a group of pupils, and discuss the results in class (Thaler 2005: 19).

Questionnaire:
Music Videos, Me and My Classroom

State your personal opinion on music videos by circling the right answer.

1. Have you ever watched music videos?
   ❑ Yes ❑ No
2. How many hours per day do you spend watching music videos?
   ❑ < 1 hour ❑ 1-2 hours ❑ > 2 hours
3. How many hours per week do you spend watching music videos?
   ❑ < 3 hours ❑ 3-6 hours ❑ > 6 hours
4. Which channel do you prefer?
   ❑ MTV ❑ VIVA ❑ …
5. Have you ever worked with music videos in the classroom?
   ❑ Yes ❑ No
6. Would you like to work with them in the English classroom?
   ❑ Yes ❑ Don't care ❑ No
7. Music videos are things that must be dealt with in an English classroom.
   ❑ Agree completely ❑ agree ❑ not sure ❑ don't agree ❑ don't agree at all
8. Using music videos in English classes helps improve my English.
   ❑ Agree completely ❑ agree ❑ not sure ❑ don't agree ❑ don't agree at all
9. Music videos are part of my private life which I do not want to discuss in class.
   ❑ Agree completely ❑ agree ❑ not sure ❑ don't agree ❑ don't agree at all
10. I do not want to work in class with videos which I do not like.
   ❑ Agree completely ❑ agree ❑ not sure ❑ don't agree ❑ don't agree at all

7 approaches

After you have selected a proper video, the next question is how to present it. This depends particularly on the peculiarities of the music video (genre, degree of popularity, topics, design) and the class aims envisaged by the teacher. Basically there are seven ways to combine the three layers of a music video, i.e. lyrics, sound, and visuals (Thaler 1999: 187, Thaler 2002: 8). The vision-off approach, for example, lends itself to videos unknown to most of the class members. Transcript and music invite pupils to speculate about the visual representation or to write a storyboard in group work. The problem that usually some pupils know the video, whereas others do not, can be turned into a virtue by resorting to the *split-version*: The first group watches the video, the second only listens to the music or reads the lyrics (*half 'n' half*); information gaps between the two halves are closed during pair work. As a rule, separating the three codes (lyrics, sound and visuals) and treating them individually avoids overloading the pupils. There is no need either to deal with all three levels, e. g. a complicated song text may be discounted in lower grades.

Music Video Approaches

Approach	*Description*
(1) Lyrics-first approach	Only the lyrics (text) are presented (handout, OHP, PPT) first. Pupils may be asked to think about characters or write a film script. Music and visuals are presented later.
(2) Sound-first approach	Only the audio track is played first. The monitor is darkened, reversed, or the pupils turn around while listening. Pupils can be asked to express their visual associations evoked by the music. Video and lyrics are presented later.
(3) Vision-first approach	The video is presented without music and lyrics. Pupils' attention is focused on viewing comprehension. Working with music and lyrics may come later.
(4) Vision-off appraoch	Pupils are given the lyrics and the soundtrack first. They may be asked to write a storyboard for the video, for example, which is compared with the video later on.
(5) Sound-off approach	The lyrics and the visuals are presented to the pupils first. The sound is turned off. Pupils may be asked to imagine rhythm, tempo, or mood of the music.
(6) Lyrics-off approach	The video (visuals plus sound) is presented without the written text. Pupils may be invited to write a stanza of their own. The lyrics can be discussed later or left out.
(7) All-codes approach	The music video is presented in its complete form (visuals, sound, written text). As this may mean asking too much of pupils' attention, different tasks can be given to various groups.

Activities

After you have decided on one of the seven approaches – or a combination of them – you have to choose suitable exercises and tasks for your learners. The following survey is based on a combination of the pre / while / post pattern and the different codes of music videos.

Music Video Activities	
Activities	*Examples*
Pre-viewing activities	• visual signs: e.g. freeze frame of singer • provocative statement: e.g. "All you need is MTV" • vote a quote: e.g. "Rock music is all make-believe" (Zappa) • pyramid discussion: e.g. "What makes life worth living: a) dance & party b) money & power c) love & romance d) reflection & meditation?" • opinion poll: e.g. "How long did you watch MTV for yesterday?" • key items: e.g. title
Text-related activities	• listening comprehension: e.g. Mondegreen version • reading comprehension: e.g. true-false statements • text analysis: e.g. speaker, characters, message, images, effect • vocabulary: e.g. paraphrases, definitions, crossword puzzle • grammar
Music-related questions	• What musical genre does this song belong to? • What effect does the rhythm have? • How does the singer interpret this song? • How would you describe the melody? • What strikes you about the music?
Visuals-related activities	• cognitive skills: e.g. describing, guessing, predicting, explaining, remembering • viewing comprehension: e.g. ticking off items from a list, upside down comprehension • film analysis: e.g. plot, characters, cinematographic devices, values, ideologies, inter-textual references, economic context, symbols, genre
Context-related activities	Questions / discussions on history, economy, form, contents, addressee, cultural critique
Integrative activities	Exploring the relationship between visuals, music, lyrics (and context)

Post-viewing tasks	• alternative ending • different person's perspective • transforming into short story • writing a review • interview with singer • debate • lip-synching • collage • video magazine • producing one's own music video

Literal music videos

Film analysis is one of the areas very well suited for a special subtype of music videos, i.e. literal music videos (see above). They have new lyrics dubbed over those of the original video, and often include captions for better clarity. Lyrics range from references to the video editing ("Now zoom in on me") to questioning the unusual things depicted in the video ("What's happening with that monkey?"). In particular, they contain a lot of cinematic techniques (camera distances, angles, movement, lighting), which can be discussed in a relaxed setting. Some of the finest and funniest examples of literal video versions – most of which are based on music videos from the 1980s and 1990s – are *Total Eclipse of the Heart* (Bonnie Tyler) and *Take on Me* (A-Ha). Finally students can be told to write their own "literal-style" texts to go with the videos, which is likely to be a rather entertaining experiment.

Favourite video presentation

Another suggestion that has proved to be a stimulating classroom experience is "My favourite music video": Individually or in small groups, students present a clip of their own choice and work on it during (part of) a lesson. To prepare them for actually teaching their clip (*learning by teaching* method), they must be equipped with a list of possible exercises and tasks (*scaffolding*).

Media education

Music videos are also an appropriate medium for the aim of film education (chapter 2.4). A discussion based on the following quotes can raise awareness about the sort of criticism often directed at music videos: glorification of fashion and technology, speed, fun, fake; capitalist consumerism and cheap mass production; mass images replacing our own fantasies set to music; commercialisation of rock music etc. (Thaler 2005: 23):

- *The message is BUY.* (D. Tetzlaff)
- *95 % of all music videos is crap – because 95 % of everything is crap.* (K. Richards)
- *MTV: Male Television, Murderous Television, Misogyny Television.* (S. Denisoff)
- *The video tail is wagging the musical dog.* (S. Levy)
- *MTV is the instant replay of bourgeois society.* (H. Hardt)
- *Music videos project images on the wall of Plato's cave since MTV took it over.* (Allan Bloom)

Witty manuals

Critical media awareness can also be promoted in an even more light-hearted way by studying how-to manuals, e. g. how to make a rap video (Thaler 2002, http://musicvideo.about.com):

How to Make a Rap Video

Here's how:

1. Get yourself a 'hood.
2. Round up a posse.
3. If male, either shave your head, wear dreadlocks, or get a cap. Females, get a hot hairdo.
4. Buy a good supply of Tommy Hilfiger clothes. If female, bulk up on the tight fitting, revealing outfits.
5. Guys, accessorize with lots of big pieces of gold jewelry. Gals, get those nails done.
6. Get an inexpensive hand-held video camera.
7. Surround yourself with plenty of suggestively dressed women. Gals, skip this step.
8. Set up the shots at those special spots in your 'hood, like the basketball court, favorite corner, or public library (just kidding on that one).
9. Include lots of 'in-your-face' close-ups.
10. Be sure to include plenty of finger-pointing hand gestures.
11. Scowl and look angry a lot. Ladies can also look sultry and pouty.
12. Process the film for that homey, grainey look.

Tips:

1. Be careful what 'hood you choose, or you may not make it back from the shoot.
2. Be sure your posse doesn't look better than you.

Which of the seven types of presentation and which of the activities mentioned above you choose, of course, depends on the specific video and the learning aims. However, busy teachers may find some assistance and comfort in a lesson plan which can be adapted to (nearly) any music video (see below: 3.3).

3.3 Lessons

Sample 1

Title	(Nearly) any music video
Length	A few minutes
Synopsis	A song with a video which is unknown to most of the students (*vision off approach*), possibly a dance music video
Topics	Any
Level	Intermediate – advanced
Time	45 or 90 minutes

Procedure:

1st step
Introduction (short teacher information)
Today let's talk about a music video. But first let's listen to the music only.

2nd step
Playing the music (DVD, Web Channel)
(*vision off approach:* monitor darkened or turned around)

3rd step
Describing the music (teacher – student discussion):
- *Do you like this music? Why (not)?*
- *What genre does this song belong to? Why?*
- *How would you describe the mood of this music: desperate – fast – relaxed – soft?*

4th step
Visualising the music (pair work):
- *What could the setting and plot of the video be like?*
- *Compare your predictions with those of your neighbour.*
- *Present your results to the class and justify your suggestions.*

5th step
Playing the music video (with visuals)

6th step
Describing the video orally:
- *What's the setting of this video?*
- *Describe the story-line.*

7th step
Comparing the music video with one's own personal associations:
What parallels and differences are there between the video and your predictions?

8th step
Critical analysis of the music video:
- *stereotypes, cliches*
- *straining after effect, razzmatazz*
- *message, intended emotions*

9th step
Handing out a worksheet with the lyrics, checking comprehension

10th step
Critical analysis of the lyrics: triteness etc.

11th step
Transfer (homework): *How can you tell a good music video from a bad one? Write a comment on that issue.*

Sample 2

Title	*Empire State of Mind* by Alicia Keys
Length	4 minutes
Synopsis	The song expresses the singer's passion for New York. Lots of places in the Big Apple are shown in the video.
Topics	New York, giving directions, adjectives for describing moods, places, music
Level	Intermediate
Time	90 (or 45) minutes

Procedure:

A. Pre-viewing phase
   1. T shows a poster of New York and asks: "What do you know about NY"? ➤ brainstorming, mindmap on blackboard / OHP / whiteboard (alternative: current news about NY)

2. T: "Have you been to NY? Would you like to go there?" ➤ T-S talk
3. T introduces Alicia Keys and hands out text on her (worksheet: cf. below) ➤ silent reading, comprehension check

B. While-viewing phase
1. T plays the video for the first time ➤ S fill in the gaps, answers are checked, unknown vocabulary is explained
2. Second (guided) viewing: "Which places / things described in the song are shown in the video?" ➤ S take notes, answers are collected in class

C. Post-viewing phase
1. "How is the city presented in the video? What's the music like? How do the music and the pictures make you feel? Do you share Alicia's feelings as described in the song?" ➤ class discussion
2. "Look at the map. Can you find the places mentioned in the song or shown in the video? Mark them." ➤ individual work
3. "Where would you like to go? Choose some places on your map (e. g. www.citimaps.com/manhattan/maps/ManhattanFull.pdf) and make a cross there (e.g. at the Guggenheim Museum). Afterwards, tell your partner which spots you have chosen for your private sightseeing tour and ask where they want to go from there. Give him / her directions. Then it's your partner's turn." ➤ pair work: asking for and giving directions

(4. and 5. possibly as homework)

4. "What do you think about the sentence 'If I can make it here, I can make it anywhere'? Do you agree? Why (not)? Write down your ideas."
5. "What do you think is an 'Empire State of Mind'? Jot down your associations."

Let's go to New York!

Alicia Keys is a native New Yorker. She had a tough childhood in the Manhattan neighbourhood Hell's Kitchen, close to Broadway and Times Square – New York's theatre district. The area used to be poor and was full of crime and gangs. But as Alicia explained to the New York magazine Gotham, things have changed since she lived there.

"It's amazing to see a neighbourhood change. When I was growing up, it was the place where all the outcasts lived. Now, it's a tourist destination – really interesting. But one thing that it always had was those bright lights and endless possibilities, because Broadway was so close. Broadway was a lot more creative and interesting."

Abb. 3 | Alicia Keys: Empire State of Mind

Alicia went to the Professional Performing Arts School, where kids learn to be stars. The school is on West 48th Street, which runs through Broadway. Alicia also used to live in Harlem, the African-American district north of Central Park. Now she lives in SoHo, South of Houston Street, at the southern end of Manhattan, near the Brooklyn Bridge.

Her song is not the only famous one about New York. Alicia refers to Frank Sinatra and his song "New York, New York" (released in 1980) when she sings "If I can make it here, I can make it anywhere". But her song is also about everyday life. For example, she sings about gypsy cabs, the unlicensed taxis that drive around the city in addition to the official, licensed yellow cabs.

Vocabulary list

English	*English explanation*	*Mother tongue*
native	born and raised in a certain place	
Gotham	a nickname for New York	
outcast	a person who does not have a lot of friends	
destination	a place where tourists want to go	
performing arts	drama, music, dance etc.	
to release	to publish	
to make it	to manage to do sth.	

Alicia Keys: **Empire State of Mind** (Part II)

Grew up in a town that is famous as the place of ______________ (a)

Noise is always loud, there are ______________ (b) all around

And the streets are mean

If I can make it here, I can make it anywhere, that's what they say

Seeing my face in lights or my name in marquees found down on

______________ (c)

Even if it ain't all it seems, I got a pocket full of dreams

Baby, I'm from New York

Concrete jungle where dreams are ______________ (d)

There's nothing you can't do

Now you're in New York

These streets will make you feel ______________ (e)

Big lights ______________ (f) you

Let's hear it for New York, New York, New York!

______________ (g), there ain't never a curfew, ladies work so hard

Such a ______________ (h), on the corner selling rock, preachers

pray to God

Hail a gypsy cab, takes me down from Harlem to the

______________ (i)

Some will sleep tonight with a hunger for more than an empty fridge

I'm gonna make it ______________ (j), I got a pocket full of dreams

Baby, I'm from New York

Concrete jungle ...

One hand in the air for the big city,

Street lights, big dreams all ______________________ (k)

No place in the world that can ______________________ (l)

Put your ______________________ (m) in the air,

everybody say yeah, yeah, yeah, yeah ... New York

Concrete jungle ...

Vocabulary List

state of mind: your mood

marquee (US): an advertising sign above a theatre / cinema entrance

concrete: building material made by mixing cement with sand, gravel, etc. and water

curfew: closing time

rock: slang word for a very dangerous drug

to hail a cab: to signal a taxi driver to stop

Tasks

1. Name and explain the different approaches to working with music videos.
2. Take the sample lesson on Alicia Keys' *Empire State of Mind*: First watch and listen to the song and do the two while-viewing tasks. Then answer post-viewing questions 1, 4, and 5.
3. Explain which video you could use to talk about a topic of your choice.

4 Commercials

When a film on TV is interrupted by commercials, which of the three options do you usually take: leave the room, zap to another channel, or stay seated? Explain why.

4.1 Theory

Definition

A commercial advertisement on television (or ad-film, TV advert) is a TV spot produced and paid for by an organization, which markets a product, service, or idea. It ranges in length from a few seconds to half a minute, sometimes even several minutes. Advertising revenue constitutes a major portion of the funding for most television networks. The audience of TV programming (measured by companies like Nielsen Media Research), is usually used as a metric for TV advert placement – and consequently for the rates charged to advertisers to air their spots.

History

Commercials have been used to promote a wide variety of products since the dawn of TV, and have quickly become the most effective mass-market advertising format. The first ad-film lasted 10 seconds and was broadcast in the US in 1941 during a baseball game (watchmaker Bulova paid $ 9). Sports programmes are still one of the most coveted environments for advertising, and the annual Super Bowl, the biggest sport event in the world, is known not only for the football game itself, but also the incredible cost of a single 30-second TV spot during this game (US$ 3 million).

Characteristics

As the primary function of commercials is to make viewers buy a product, they rely on certain features and strategies. Based on Lasswell's famous formula of mass communication ("Who says What in Which Channel to Whom with What Effect?") and the long-established AIDA formula (Attention – Interest – Desire – Action), the following characteristics can often be identified (e. g. Henseler / Möller / Surkamp 2011: 193ff.):

Characteristics of Commercials	
Features	*Examples*
Targeting selected audiences	teenage products during commercial breaks in sitcoms
Targeting selected milieus	lifestyle spots for self-fulfilment milieu (Knobloch / Raab 2002: five types of spots = five social milieus)
Surprise effects	tricks, parodies, JELL-O: free pudding for San Francisco (after 2013 Super Bowl): "bringing you the sweet taste of pudding to mask the bitter taste of defeat."
Intensifiers	superlatives (greatest, best, cheapest), hyperbole (mega cool)
Testimonials	experts, celebrities, personalities representing the targeted group
Scientific evidence	statistics, charts, graphs, lab coats, libraries
Bandwagon	... everybody is doing it ... if you buy it, you are on the "winning team" ...
Beautiful people	... If we buy the product we'll look like the models ...
Stereotyping	man as hero / / urban man / family man / consumer / outdoors man / quiescent
Popular songs	Budweiser 2013 Super Bowl TV spot: *Brotherhood* by Fleetwood Mac
Jingles (short melodies)	"I'd like to teach the world to sing." (Coke)
Slogans (catch-phrases)	Just do it. (Nike) I don't want to grow up. (Toys 'R' Us)
Animation	traditional and computer-generated, Kit Kat: vending machine
Simplifications	Power is Macintosh. (Apple) *card-stacking* in movie ads
Claims	beauty, novelty, quality, efficiency, simplicity, safety, stability, utility
Appealing to needs	need for sex / affiliation / attention, need to achieve / nurture / dominate
Symbols	2013 Mercedes Super Bowl ad: lots of devil's symbols
Humour	Puns with sexual innuendo: "After you get married, kiss your wife in places she's never been kissed before." (ad for honeymoon destinations)

Meaning

As to the meaning of commercials, Frith (1998: 5) adopts a tripartite approach to reading advertising:

- surface meaning: "... consists of the overall impression that a reader might get from quickly studying the advertisement ... you can describe this surface level of meaning by simply listing all the objects and people in the ad" (ibid.).

- intended meaning: "... the sales message that the advertiser is trying to get across ... the strategy behind the ad ... the 'preferred' or expected meaning ..." (ibid.).
- cultural or ideological meaning: "... relies on the cultural knowledge and background ... we all 'make sense' of ads by relating them to our culture and to the shared belief systems held in common by most people" (ibid.).

Whereas the first layer is obvious, the second and third are often quite hard for viewers – and our students – to decode.

Rationale

Commercials are self-contained clips which contain a high level of repetition. This repetition as well as their brevity aid comprehension and make ads suitable for younger learners as well. They are professionally made with every word and cinematic device being purposeful and precise, which makes them multifaceted objects of analysis. The content is often intriguing or funny, the language idiomatic and authentic, and the twists of the plot sometimes confuse our minds.

"They have shock, beauty, atmosphere, glamour, drama, comedy, all in the space of 15 – 30 seconds" (Sherman 2003: 105). And they are often targeted at children and teenagers, who constitute a profitable target group for industry. Revealing persuasive strategies in advertising thus becomes a necessary learning objective.

Criticism

Whatever entertainment value beyond the basic message some of them have, and however vital for economic growth they may be regarded, commercials, however, face a lot of criticism by viewers, for example:

- sub-conscious influence: profit-minded companies manipulate customers to buy their products.
- false needs: commercials entice people to buy things they do not need or want.
- psychological pressure: for example, ads appeal to feelings of inadequacy.
- nuisance: people find ads annoying; they often cut into parts of the regular programming, which are exciting or entertaining to watch.

4.2 Methodology

Sources

To get hold of a proper ad in good quality used to be a serious problem 15 years ago, but in the Internet era we have access to different web-based platforms opening up a great variety of samples and ways to work with them:

- www.youtube.com
- www.google.com/videohp
- www.visit4info.com/
- www.adforum.com/
- www.veryfunnyads.com
- www.esm.psu.edu/faculty/gray/movies.html
- www.tellyads.com/

And should the teacher still be unable to find the right sample, he / she can go directly to the advertising department of the product.

Selection criteria

To decide whether a commercial is suitable for a class or not, teachers have to study its content and relate it to the competences they are aiming at. Sometimes a spot is too culture-bound, or provocative, or simply has too little learning potential. The following table, which distinguishes between three levels, can help to choose the right commercial for one's class (Henseler / Möller / Surkamp 2011: 197).

Selection Criteria

Levels	*Content*	*Aspects / competences*
Lower grades	Content for 10-13-year olds: common products, narrative commercials, subjects relating to topics in textbooks	Watch and speak, watch and write, small observing tasks
Intermediate grades	Content for 13-15 year-olds: products from pupils' everyday lives, commercials for campaigns (no drugs, health, public service announcements)	Watch and speak, watch and write, critical perspective tasks, more complex ways of watching the ad, talking about genre and institutions
Senior grades	Content for 15-20-year olds: election campaign ads, new ideas, current issues	Complex observing and research tasks, detailed analysis of language, techniques, intertextuality

Activities

Commercials are suitable for numerous kinds of activities (Sherman 2003, Stempleski / Tomalin 2001): grids for comprehension questions, repetition exercises and sound-off dubbing for phonetic improvement, lexical and structural work (synonyms, antonyms, collocations, e. g. noun plus adjective), frame-by-frame description, prediction, sound-off for writing tasks and guessing the music, comparison with magazine ads, and producing a videotaped advert.

Massler's approach

A very comprehensive approach to working with commercials has been propounded by Ute Massler (2006). Although the examples focus on football clips, her general suggestions can be applied for any commercial. Her set of ideas is grouped into four levels:

A) Exploiting the language

1. Lead-in activities
- Introducing relevant expressions (brainstorming, making a cluster)
- Pre-teaching key-words, slang / colloquial expressions used in the commercial
- Providing contextual help, e.g. who is talking, where, why
- Handing out a transcript (complete or with gaps or scrambled up) for difficult commercials: students read it, work on vocabulary

2. Comprehension activities
- Reading transcript (and filling in gaps) or checking order of the scrambled up transcript while viewing the commercial
- Information exchange: pairs of learners watch a commercial, one concentrates on what one specific person says / does, they then exchange what they found out
- Silent viewing: Showing images only, students speculate on what actors say, then check when sound is added

3. Follow-up activities
- Retelling the commercial from an actor's point of view
- Giving actors a voice or providing a comment (for commercials without spoken text): writing a text (dialogue, inner monologue, or commentator's voice), acting it out
- Producing a dubbed German version of an English commercial

- Finding sub-titles for videos without spoken text, holding text underneath the TV screen
- Writing one's own commercials

B) Exploiting the commercial

1. Lead-in activities ➤ first insight into the economy, form and content of commercials

- Introducing basic knowledge: Discussing commercials from three different perspectives using up-to-date examples students know from TV:
  - Economic perspective: Who finances commercials? What types of products are most likely to be advertised?
  - Artistic perspective: Are commercials visually gratifying? Are they enjoyable to watch?
  - Meaning: Which are the surface, which the subliminal messages? How do commercials function?
- Alerting students to the specific production of a certain subtype of commercials: Students are told the name and kind of product; they then discuss what kind of ad they expect and write down five words they would expect to hear / see.

2. Analysis

The following table summarizes typical analysis questions, which then have to be selected and adapted according to the learner's level.

Analysis Questions

(Massler 2006, Frith 1998, Henseler / Möller / Surkamp 2011)

I. Product

- What product is advertised?
- When is the product shown (beginning, middle, end, not at all)?

II. Narrative

- What story-line can you detect?
- How is the narrative structured?
- How are characters depicted?
- Why has this model / actor been chosen?
- What does the setting / context / location signify?

III. Techniques
- What cinematic devices are used (camera angles, movement etc.)? Why?
- What is the pace of the commercial?
- How does the lighting help create a mood?
- What colours are used and why?

IV. Sound
- How do sounds affect the viewer?
- Does the ad make use of a jingle?
- What is the function of the voice-over?
- How does music grab our attention?
- What kind of language is used?

V. Audience
- Who is the target audience? Who are the advertisers trying to reach?
- What image do the producers associate with their costumers?
- How does the commercial represent a particular social group (**representation**)?
- Is this representation accurate, realistic, distorted?

VI. Strategies
- What advertising strategies are used?
- What claims are made about the product?
- What needs are appealed to?
- What image are the advertisers trying to give the product?
- How does the commercial try to catch our attention?
  - ➤ via a new selling-point (e. g. more effective product than before, difference between haves and have-nots, before and after using the product, ...)
  - ➤ via a new way of selling (e. g. a joke)
  - ➤ by arousing curiosity (e. g. not showing the product until the very end)
  - ➤ by parodying media programmes (e. g. action movies)
  - ➤ by 'borrowing' a mission from a fashionable cause (e. g. the environment)
  - ➤ by using *anchoring* techniques (e. g. jingles, slogans, animation, sound)

VII. Meaning
- What message does the commercial convey on the surface?
- What seems to be the intended meaning? How is it related to the product?
- Can you identify any cultural or ideological meaning?

VIII. Impact
- How effective is the commercial?
- Will it have the desired effect on viewers?
- What might make it better?

3. Follow-up activities
- Evaluating and comparing commercials
- Fostering discussion skills by introducing appropriate language: e. g. downtoners (to soften questions, statements, negative responses)
- Awarding commercials: students assess and give reasons for ranking, vote for their favourite commercial, write their own top ten list, develop a rating scale
- Researching the Internet for products / services advertised in the commercial or for actors that perform in it

C) Exploiting the culture

- Exploring the personalities starring in the commercial
- Discussing intercultural aspects

D) Bringing it all together

The creativity of commercials may incite learners to become creators themselves (Chee 1994: 155). The knowledge and skills acquired on the first three levels (A, B and C) via professional commercials, are now applied when producing their own amateur clip.
- Making your own commercial: students select one genre, develop a script, practise and videotape it; then they present and grade each other's commercials based on the following (Davis 1997): a) originality, b) use of English, c) persuasive arguments demonstrating knowledge of the subject, d) presentation skills (delivery)
- Producing a commercial series: students watch a certain clip and write a follow-up commercial which uses the same design elements; presenting and grading via criteria as before (plus: similarity to original)

4.3 Lessons

Sample 1

Title	Vizzavi – Pixar Tennis Chicks
Length	30 seconds
Synopsis	Two young chickens watch their parents play tennis. One of the youngsters is mistaken for the tennis ball. The other immediately informs all of their friends about the funny mistake via smart phone.
Topics	Advertising techniques, communication, sports, humour
Level	Beginners / intermediate
Time	45 minutes, without part C 4-7 (3 to 4 lessons for complete unit)

Procedure:

A. Pre-viewing

1. What do you usually do during commercial breaks? Why?
2. Are there any commercials you enjoy watching? Which ones? Why?

B. While-viewing

Freeze frame after the opening scene when the tennis ball rolls towards the young chickens and comes to a stop next to them:

1. *Describing*: Which animals did you spot? Where are they? What are they doing?
2. *Analysing*: Has the first scene aroused your attention and interest? Why?
3. *Predicting*: How might the story go on?

C. Post-viewing

1. *Describing the product*: What product does the commercial want to sell? Why should someone buy it?
2. *Analysing the strategies*: Who is the commercial trying to attract (What is the target group)? Teenagers or adults? How can you tell?
3. *Transforming strategies into general advertising rules*: Work with your partner. Collect ideas of what you think makes a TV commercial successful.

Suggested answers:

a) attracts the interest of a target audience (female / male, young / old)
b) arouses emotions
c) provides information about the product's features (Why is it unique?)
d) uses exaggerations
e) is often humorous
f) is short (30 seconds – 2 minutes).

g) ______________________________

h) ______________________________

4. *Commercial project*: Students get together in groups and create their own TV commercial with the help of a short checklist:

a) The product
– What sort of product do you want to sell?
– Why should someone need your product?
– What makes your product unique?

b) Scripting your commercial
– Remember the points that make a successful TV commercial.
– Make sure that everybody in your group has an acting part.

c) Materials and props
– What materials do you need for decoration?
– Who brings which materials?
– Do you want to use costumes?
– Who brings which costumes?

d) Don't forget:
– to finish your scripts
– to bring all costumes and materials needed
– to learn the text for your role

5. *Acting + Voting*: Every group performs their invented commercial in class. The other students do a while-viewing-activity, the *ticket vote*: Students throw their tickets with the performing group's name on it into one of two boxes (good – okay).
6. *Awarding*: Group with the commercial voted best is awarded a small prize.
7. *Discussing*: Why was the commercial of Group X voted the best? Which ideas for a successful TV commercial did they use?

Sample 2

Title	Super Bowl project
Length	Several clips of varying length
Synopsis	The Super Bowl is a sports event that draws most media attention, at least in the US, and consequently the most expensive (and often very creative) commercials are aired during the event. A short research project may try to reveal the background of this event.
Topics	Sport, business, companies, prime time, cinematic techniques, media literacy
Level	Intermediate – advanced
Time	3 lessons

Procedure:

1. Lead-in
   – introducing the topic
   – pointing out the importance of the event

2. Forming groups
   Group A: background I
   Guiding questions:
   1. What do you know about the Super Bowl game?
   2. Why does this match get such tremendous media attention every year?
   3. What makes advertisers want to put their ads on air during this once-a-year sports event?
   4. What does a 30-second ad cost?
   5. Why can they charge such an amount of money?
   6. Which ad would you be looking forward to seeing? Why?

Group B: commercial 1
   Choose one of the Super Bowl ads and analyse the following aspects:
   product, narrative, techniques, sound, audience, strategies, meaning, impact.

Group C: commercial 2 (see above)

Group D: commercial 3 (see above)

Group E: background II
   Guiding questions:
   1. Who decides what order the ads air during the match?
   2. How do advertisers create a buzz about their commercials even before the match?
   3. Create a list of ads, advertisers and their parent companies.
   4. How many ads are for: alcohol, cars, movies? Why?
   5. Can you find ads inside / outside / above the stadium? If so, where? Be on the lookout for not-so-obvious ads during the broadcast.
   6. How do advertisers make money from their Super Bowl spots?

3. Group work (classroom, computer room, at home)

4. Presenting and discussing the results

5. Final evaluation

Sample 3

The online video platform www.englishcentral.com provides commercials prepared for language learning, to use for free in class or at home. Teachers can work with their students on listening and reading comprehension, spelling, pronunciation, and vocabulary. They get a completely designed unit based on one video each.
1. Watch: The bar at the bottom of the clip shows every word spoken during the commercial as subtitles, supporting the students' understanding of difficult words and helping them improve on their spelling skills.
Students are able to click on every word in order to obtain further information.
As soon as the student clicks on one of the words, another window pops up and shows the correct definition, phonetic transcription, sample sentence as well as a button for repeating the pronunciation.
2. Learn: In part 2, the commercial is stopped at certain points, and students have to type in the missing words they have just heard. They may rewind and listen again.
3. Speak: In the last section, students are able to speak the words using a microphone. The speaker in the commercial says the word first, then the video stops, and students can repeat.

Tasks

1. What are the three layers of meaning according to Katherine Frith?
2. Choose a commercial, and try to identify those three dimensions of meaning.
3. *The Snowman Journey* (2012) is a Christmas commercial by the John Lewis department stores, and has become one of the most popular spots. Watch it online, and decide whether you would use it in class (http://www.youtube.com/watch?v=oN8axp9nHNU). Afterwards you may take a look behind the scenes at the making of the John Lewis Christmas advert: www.youtube.com/watch?v=K54f3vtVido.

5 Sketches

Watch a sketch from the British cult series *Little Britain*, e. g. one of the *Computer Says 'No'* clips (www.youtube.com/watch?v=qNDS4kVwA68):

- Do you personally like the sketch? Explain why (not).
- Are you going to use it in your classrooms? Why (not)?

5.1 Theory

History

The genre of sketches has its origins in vaudeville and music hall in the late 19th and early 20th century, where a large number of short, humorous acts were joined together to form a larger programme. The sketch gradually developed from a random collection of unrelated jokes to a well-planned short act performance with written scripts. Today, sketches are a central part of modern variety shows, comedy programmes, adult entertainment, talk shows and certain children's television series. In the UK, it moved from music hall to stage performances (e. g. *Cambridge Footlights*), to radio (e. g. *It's That Man Again*), then to television (e. g. Monty Python's *Flying Circus, Not the Nine O'Clock News*). More recent groups have introduced overarching themes connecting the sketches within a particular show, with recurring characters, for example Lou & Andy from *Little Britain*. Some feature films are composed entirely of comedy sketches such as Monty Python's *The Meaning of Life*. The most prestigious comedy prize in the UK is The Edinburgh Comedy Awards presented to the best shows at the Edinburgh Festival Fringe. Over the last 15 years, the growing sketch comedy scene has also precipitated the development of sketch comedy festivals in cities all around North America.

Terminology

A sketch is an elaborated and dramatised joke, i.e. a joke made longer and acted out between different characters. The term 'sketch' is related to the German word 'Skizze', and etymologically seems to derive from the Greek word σχέδιος (shédios), which roughly translates into 'something improvised' (Müller 2003: 266). Today though, it is not usually improvised, but written down, learned and then performed. An individual *sketch*, also called *vignette* or *skit*, is a brief scene, whereas *sketch comedy* consists of a series of short sketches. Sometimes a difference in quality is implied: skits tend to be light dramatized jokes, whereas a sketch is seen as a more ambitious comedic exploration of a certain idea.

Müller's definition

A very convincing and precise definition of sketch is propounded by Müller (2003: 274f.):

"A sketch presents a (1) fictional plot or event (2) in a dramatic way. The genre differs from other genres through its (3) low level of complexity: the plot is mostly limited to (3a) one single location or (3b) to one single action or dialogue or (3c) to two, rarely more than four protagonists. The characters are known to the recipient (4) in general outline through (4a) their model, (4b) their intertextuality or (4c) recognizable encoding. The text (5) wants to create humor by using (5a) a (in most cases closing) punch line or (5b) other instruments of entertainment (like slapstick, voice imitation, etc.) or (5c) satirical attack."

Characteristics

Deducing from this definition, one can list a few constituent features of sketches:

- Medium: very often an audio-visual one (TV, DVD, video); often performed live on stage; audio types (just for listening) and print forms (for reading)
- Restricted number of characters and settings
- Length: anything between 15 seconds and a few minutes (comedy shows on TV: usually half an hour)
- Humour: If you get a big laugh at least every fifteen seconds, you have written quite a good one.

Situations

Sketches can cover every possible situation and topic in life. They deal with strange ways of moving (Monty Python: *Ministry of Silly Walks*), a man complaining about modern technology mistaken for fruit (The One Ronnie: *My Blackberry Is Not Working!*), or a gadget mysteriously intervening with everyday life (Smosh: *Magic Keyboard*). Quite a lot of sketches fall into the following tried and tested categories (www.writerswrite.com/journal/jul99/luff.htm):

Situations in Sketches		
Situation / topic	*Description*	*Examples*
Escalation	a funny idea starting small and getting bigger and bigger	Olde English: *Pizza Delivery* (two friends watching a marathon of their favourite show, being unable to reach the phone to order food)
Risk	dangerous setting or event	David Letterman: *The Guy Who Beats up Alan Kalter*
List	the main part of the dialogue being a long list of funny items	Monty Python: *Cheese Shop*, in which thirty-plus different sorts of cheese are mentioned
Language	the sound of language, playing on words, homonymy, word fields ...	puns (e. g. German Willy Astor), word field 'to die' in Monty Python's *Dead Parrot*
Old vs new	putting something modern in an historical setting or v.v. (anachronism)	Sir Walter Raleigh using a cigarette lighter
Big vs small	relying on large differences in scale	a midget falling in love with an amazon-type of woman
Mad vs sane	... with the mad usually gaining the upper hand	Peter Cook's one-legged Tarzan sketch (or: any sketch in which two characters are diametrically opposed to each other)
Spoof	parodying a genre, person, event	mock western, space movie, historical romance

Apart from the arguments for using films in general (see ch. 1), sketches are short and funny.

Rationale

Due to their limited duration, they can be watched all the way through two or three times and exploited with several tasks even during one 45-minute lesson. The humour alone makes them worth watching, but the different forms and functions of humour can also be studied.

Problems

However, some of the general problems (see ch. 1) also apply for sketches. They sometimes use elaborate vocabulary, hard words, cultural references and rhetorical devices, e. g. puns, which are quite difficult to understand. The topics might also be inappropriate, or the students have problems understanding the punch line. Sketches often contain some sexual innuendo which, if understood, may cause some laughter among pubescent teenagers. Similar problems may result from the occasional cursing and swearing, although any YouTube-savvy teenager will have encountered this anyway.

5.2 Methodology

Sources

There are many ways to get hold of sketches from all kinds of sources. Firstly there are feature films, which may include – more or less self-contained – humorous skits, for example the discussion on "What have the Romans ever done for us?" in Monty Python's *Life of Brian*. Then, you can resort to collections of sketches on DVD, such as *Little Britain – the Complete 1st Season*. If you have access to English speaking TV channels such as BBC Entertainment, you can also record your favourite sketches for private use – and occasionally show them in the classroom. The richest source with easiest access is, of course, the Internet. Sketches can be found in no time at all via search engines like Google, video platforms like YouTube or Vimeo, or TV channels' websites like BBC.

Teenage sketch channel

One of the most established sketch channels is Smosh, currently the one with the most subscribers on YouTube. Smosh, a comedy duo, usually speak an easy-to-understand American English, the conversational dialogues are not over-sophisticated, the protagonists' typical overacting supports the spoken word and makes understanding easier, and the funny content appeals to many teenagers.

Britain's Top 10

If you favour British humour, you may take a shine to the list of Britain's most popular sketches, with *Little Britain* topping the poll, and Monty Python's legendary *Dead Parrot* coming in at number two
(http://news.bbc.co.uk/2/hi/entertainment/4406377.stm):

Britain's Top 10 Sketches

1. Little Britain: *Lou & Andy, Swimming Pool*
2. Monty Python's Flying Circus: *Dead Parrot*
3. The League of Gentlemen: *Tubbs & Edward, Road Men*
4. Little Britain: *Vicky Pollard, Swimming Pool*
5. The Two Ronnies: *Four Candles*
6. Goodness Gracious Me: *Going For An English*
7. Victoria Wood, As Seen on TV: *Acorn Antiques, Original*
8. The Morecambe & Wise Show: *Breakfast*
9. The Fast Show: *Ted & Ralph, Drinking Game*
10. Brass Eye: *Good Aids / Bad Aids*

Lesson structure

Most of the lesson patterns suggested in ch. 1 are well suited for sketches, in particular the PWP approach and the 10-step approach (see below: sample lessons). In the pre-viewing stage, it seems beneficial to take up the topic or situation of the sketch and relate it to the students' personal experiences, to pre-teach key phrases for understanding the humour (punch line), and to have learners guess about the story-line. During the while-viewing stage, the whole sketch should usually be watched without interruption to allow for pure enjoyment; a freeze frame right before the punch-line, however, with an invitation to predict the last words has proven to be an attractive task. Reasonable alternatives to normal straight-through viewing are blind listening and, in particular, silent viewing. The pause button may also be pressed during the second viewing to explain linguistic or cultural problems. The follow-up phase lends itself for questions aimed at humour analysis, and some creative activities based on the topic of the sketch.

Spontaneous responses

As the topics and sort of humour in sketches usually provoke controversial reactions, students should be encouraged to voice their personal impressions (Lütge 2012: 47f.):

- What made you laugh?
- What was most unexpected?
- What did you like / dislike?
- Did you find the presentation amusing / ridiculous / exaggerated / sad?

- Write down two characters / objects / words / events you remember.
- Jot down two spontaneous questions about the film.

5.3 Lessons

Sample 1

Title	*Magic Keyboard* (www.youtube.com/watch?v=XJ87Lsx40PI)
Length	3:10 minutes
Synopsis	One of the protagonists, Anthony, finds and uses a keyboard which enables him to manipulate the real world with common writing programme commands like copy and paste. At the end he forgets to save and shuts down the world as if it was a computer.
Topics	Computer commands, reality and fantasy, teenage lives, dreams
Level	Intermediate
Time	45 minutes

Procedure:

A. Pre-viewing
1. How often do you use your computer and what for?
2. What commands / keys do you know?
3. Let's describe the keys on a keyboard (a real one, if available; if not, a transparency).
4. Which, to your mind, is the most important command?

B. While-viewing
1. First viewing: silent viewing (sound off)
2. Global comprehension: Retell the story (class chain: each student says one sentence).
3. Second viewing (with sound)
4. Detailed comprehension: comparing story with assumptions in step 2.

C. Post-viewing
1. Evaluation: Did you like this video? Why (not)?
2. Imagining: What would you do if you had a keyboard like that?
3. Creative writing (homework): On your computer write a short story about what you would do with a magic keyboard.

Magic Keyboard (script):

[Anthony appears in a very messy room.]
A: God, where the hell are my keys? Seriously, how can anyone live in this crap?
[Ian emerges from a pile of trash stacked over him and the couch he is sitting on.]
I: What are you talking about? Every item here has its own purpose.
[Anthony shakes his head and discovers the keyboard. He picks it up and uses the find-command to find his car keys.]
I: Hey, don't mess with my stuff!
A: What stuff?
[Anthony uses the Select All command and presses Delete. The trash is gone. Ian is shocked.]
I. My treasure! My sweet sweet treasure! (crying) You'll pay for what you've done!
[Anthony takes a dollar and copy/pastes it several times, looking very excited. Ian rubs his hands cheerfully.]
I: Uuuh, Money!
[Ian jumps from the couch but falls over the table. Anthony laughs.]
I: Aaaah, God!
A: Haha, oh my...
[Anthony uses the Undo command several times to watch Ian fall over the table more times. After many falls Ian stands up.]
I: Oh my God dude, this thing is awesome! (very fast) Dude, you can like copy paste sandwiches all over the place and like eat them like everywhere you want and like chocolate bars ...
[Anthony gets annoyed with Ian's barrage and turns on music to drown his talking. When Ian continues to talk Anthony turns up the music until Ian almost cannot be heard anymore. Anthony then selects Ian.]
I: (panics) Hey, what are you doing?
[Anthony types "hot chick" in the replace folder.]
I: No, no! No, don't do that, don't do th...!
[Anthony enters and instead of Ian a pretty girl is now standing in front of him. She smiles.]
A: Hey. What do you say you and I, ehm, get outta here?
[She nods, he puts his arm around her and they leave the house where Anthony's old car stands. He looks embarrassed and she disappointed. Anthony produces the keyboard, types "crappy car" in the "find" folder and "Ferrari" in the replace folder. Anthony enters and a black Ferrari stands before them. Both look happy and take place in the car.]
A: I know this is kinda fast, but I think I'm in love with you.

G (with Ian's voice): I think I love you too!
A: (confused). Why do you still have Ian's voice?
G: What are you talking about?
A: Your voice! Why is it still...
G: Shut up and kiss me already!
A: D... no!
[Anthony tries the Undo command several times but it only resets to the "Shut up and kiss me already". After a few attempts the display reads: Cannot undo any further.]
A: Sh*bleeped* close, close, close, close!
[He presses Ctrl-Alt-Del frantically. The keyboard displays "Force shut down". Behind him a windows screen appears and the Windows XP-shut down tune plays.]
A: Dammit!
[The screen goes black for a second, then Antony reappears standing alone, around him is plain white nothingness.]
A: Oh, great. Well I guess I just open an old save.
[He presses a button on the keyboard and an "Open" folder appears, but below it reads "No save files".]
A: Wha... I forgot to save? (breaks down dramatically) I always forget to save!
[The screen zooms out and a Windows bluescreen appears.]

Sample 2

Title	*Fatal Beatings* (www.youtube.com/watch?v=YBeguUvuDzs) Version with subtitles: http://www.youtube.com/watch?v=EgOvNJeefvA (mistakes to be corrected: 0:25: "I'd like to nip it in the bud" 0:40: "muck in" 1:15: "out on his ear" 1:21: "sick bay")
Length	3 minutes 54 seconds
Synopsis	Rowan Atkinson stars as a conceited, authoritarian schoolmaster, who matter-of-factly states to the father of a student that he has beaten his son to death for taking out library books without library cards ...

Topics	School, headmaster – parents relationship, British black humour, discipline, punishment
Level	Upper intermediate – advanced
Time	90 minutes (or 45: without follow-up options)

Procedure:

A. Pre-viewing
1. Have you ever had to face any school sanctions? Which ones? Why?
2. In what cases is it justified to expel a pupil from school?

B. Viewing – in three parts
1. First freeze frame after "Dear me": What would you do to stop such behaviour if you were the headmaster?
2. Second freeze frame before last line: What might be the headmaster's last words?
3. After the end: checking global comprehension (class discussion)
(4. possibly a second viewing with the subtitled version)

C. Follow-up
In pairs, students choose one or two of the following five tasks (*Freiarbeit*):
1. Media transfer: Turn the sketch (dialogue) into a newspaper article for the yellow press.
2. Selection: Choose three funny lines / passages and explain why they are humorous.
3. Comparison: Compare the spoken text with its subtitles. (additional viewing necessary, for mistakes in the subtitles: see above)
4. Creating text: Delete the ending and write an alternative one.
5. Language analysis: Paraphrase these idioms in English and translate them into your mother tongue: *to nip it in the bud, to muck in, to make allowances for the fact, to be out on one's ear, to pull one's leg.*

Fatal Beatings (script)

Headmaster: Well now, Mr. Perkins. It was good of you to come in. I realise that you're a busy man, but I didn't think this matter could be discussed over the electric telephone.
Mr Perkins: No. No, absolutely, Headmaster, I mean, if Tommy is in some sort of trouble, then I'd like to nip it in the bud.
Headmaster: Well, quite frankly, Tommy is in trouble. Recently, his behaviour has left a great deal to be desired.
Mr Perkins: Dear me!
Headmaster: He seems to take no interest in school life whatsoever. He refuses to muck in on the sports field. And it's weeks since any master has received any written work from him.
Mr Perkins: Oh, dear me.
Headmaster: Quite frankly, Mr Perkins, if he wasn't dead, I'd have him expelled.
Mr Perkins: I beg your pardon?
Headmaster: Yes, EXPELLED! If I wasn't making allowances for the fact that your son is dead, he'd be out on his ear!
Mr Perkins: You mean he's dead?
Headmaster: Yes ... He's lying up there in sick bay now, stiff as a board and bright green, and this is, I fear, typical of his current attitude. You see, the boy has no sense of moderation: one moment he's flying around like a paper kite, and the next moment he's completely immovable. And beginning to smell.
Mr Perkins: Well, how did he die?!
Headmaster: Well, is that important?
Mr Perkins: Why, yes, I think so!
Headmaster: Well ... Well ... Well, it's all got to do with the library, you see. We've had a lot of trouble recently with boys taking out library books without library cards. Your son was caught, and I administered a beating, during which he died. But you'll be glad to know ... You'll be glad to know that the ringleader was caught, so I don't think we'll be having any trouble with library discipline. You see, the library card system ...
Mr Perkins: I'm sorry ...
Headmaster: ... was ...
Mr Perkins: You beat my son to death?
Headmaster: Yes, yes, so it would seem. Please, I'm not used to being interrupted. You see, the library card system was introduced ...
Mr Perkins: Well, exactly what happened?
Headmaster: Well, apparently, boys were just slipping into the library and taking the books!

Mr Perkins: No, during the beating!
Headmaster: Oh, that? Well ... well, one moment he was bending over, the next moment he was lying down, I mean, er ...
Mr Perkins: Dead?
Headmaster: Mmm ... deadish! ... Mr.Perkins, I find this morbid fascination with your son's death quite disturbing. What I'm talking about is his attitude! And quite frankly, I can see where he gets it from.
Mr Perkins: Well, it wasn't me that beat my son to death!
Headmaster: Well, that was perfectly obvious to me from the first day he arrived here. I wondered then, as I wonder now, if he might not have turned out a very different boy indeed if you had administrated a few fatal beatings earlier.
Mr Perkins: Are you mad!?
Headmaster: I'm FURIOUS! In order to accommodate the funeral, I had to cancel afternoon school on Wednesday!
Mr Perkins: This is preposterous!
Headmaster: Yes, it is. Or at least, it would be ... if it were true.
Mr Perkins: ...What?
Headmaster: I've been joking, Mr Perkins. Pardon me, it's my strange academic sense of humour. I've been pulling your leg.
Mr Perkins: Oh, thank God!
Headmaster: I wouldn't cancel afternoon school to bury that little shit!

www.wepsite.de/Fatal%20Beatings%28sketch%29.htm

Sample 3

Title	Monty Python's: *Dead Parrot* (or: *In the Pet Shop*) (www.youtube.com/watch?v=4vuW6tQ0218, stopping after 3.00: ... till you're blue in the mouth) Preferably with subtitles: www.youtube.com/watch?v=RQhVLHu8HRk (including a few mistakes)
Length	3 minutes
Synopsis	Maybe the most famous sketch in the history of British television comedy, *Dead Parrot* shows Mr Praline entering a pet shop to register a complaint about a dead Norwegian Blue parrot he has just bought. The proprietor insists that it is "pining for the fjords" or simply "stunned". The exasperated Praline attempts to wake up the parrot, bangs "Polly Parrot" on the counter, and finally lists off several metaphors for 'death'.

Topics		Shopkeeper – customer relations, complaining, service industries, British humour, communication strategies (convincing, distracting), word fields, register
Level		Advanced
Time		90 minutes (or 45': without 3rd viewing, reducing step 10)
Step	Function	Procedure
1	Raising motivation for listening-viewing	• Let's watch the most popular sketch in the world. • Situation: In the pet shop, owner and buyer of parrot
2	Pre-teaching	• Explaining a few key phrases • Introducing Monty Python's
3	Setting the first intention	Purpose: global understanding
4	First viewing	Presenting the whole sketch (with subtitles)
5	Checking global comprehension	Spot the lies: This summary of the sketch contains five mistakes. Underline them and correct them. *A customer, Mr Praline, enters a toy shop to register a complaint about the sick parrot which he had bought a few weeks before. The female shopkeeper, who is just preparing to close the establishment for lunch, disagrees with the customer. Mr Praline gets more and more furious as the shopkeeper tries to distract him with all sorts of excuses. Right to the end, he is not willing to take it back.* a) ____________________ b) ____________________ c) ____________________ d) ____________________ e) ____________________

6	Setting the second intention	Read the following tasks before you watch a second time: a) How does the customer try to convince the shopkeeper that the parrot is dead? Name three strategies. b) How does the shopkeeper distract the customer? List three strategies.
7	Second viewing	Presenting the sketch a 2nd time
8	Checking detailed under-standing	Discussing the two tasks a) and b) above (Step 6)
9	Focused 3rd viewing	• 3rd viewing: end of sketch • Guiding task: Try to remember at least five words for 'to die'. • Working on register: word field 'to die' on blackboard (columns: legal, religious, theatre, general) • Filling in the four columns
10	Follow-up	Elaborating on comprehension: a) Pythonesque Humour: When did you laugh? Why? b) Role play: One pupil wants to exchange a faulty object (mobile, notebook ...), the other tries to reject it. Work in pairs, write down the dialogue, and act it out. c) Creative writing: Write a sketch about your teacher and yourself. You try to talk your way out of having forgotten your homework. (If you forget this homework, you will have to perform the sketch in class.)

Tasks

1. Distinguish between the terms *sketch*, *skit*, and *sketch comedy* by referring to the historic background.
2. Watch Monty Python's *Dead Parrot* and do tasks 8, 9, and 10a) of the lesson plan above.
3. Take a sketch of your choice (e. g. from Britain's Top Ten), and design a 45-minute lesson plan based on the 10-step approach (see above).

Medium Formats

6 Sitcoms

- What sitcoms do you watch?
- Are they suitable for English language classrooms?

6.1 Theory

Definition

The term *sitcom* is a blend word for 'situation comedy', suggesting that the main source of humour lies in the intricacies of varying situations, which are often presented in exaggerated and stereotypical ways (e. g. Gunzenhäuser / Hahn 2009). Every episode of a sitcom lasts about 30 minutes (frequent advertising breaks reducing the length down to 24 minutes), and is self-contained, i.e. events resolve themselves within one episode. *Soap operas* (*soaps*), in contrast, are marked by the open-ended nature of the narrative, with episodes often ending on a *cliff-hanger*, and stories spanning several episodes. In both formats, the viewer recognizes the same setting and the same central characters, who are exposed to new (comic) situations. The stories are often *centred narratives*, i.e. based around an individual or a pair, with other characters subordinated to the protagonist(s). The number of both characters and settings (work-based, domestic, leisure-time environments) is rather restricted compared to feature films. Most sitcoms feature recorded laughter, which is either taped with a live audience in the studio or afterwards during a screening of the episode. Another characteristic is the running gag, i.e. an amusing joke or a comical reference which appears repeatedly throughout a series (e. g. Kenny's frequent death in *South Park*).

Critique

Of course, sitcoms (and soap operas) are easy prey for intellectuals devoted to cultural critique (Thaler 2005). In their view, sitcoms ...

- distract us from the essential
- glorify triviality
- corrupt our ethical sense
- dull our minds
- endanger the young.

Popularity

Yet, the enormous popularity of these types of programmes with teenagers (and – on the quiet – university graduates) must have its reasons. "Soap opera has been the most popular form of television programme in Britain for 40 years since the first episode of *Coronation Street* was screened in 1960" (Düwel / von der Grün 2001: 94). Is it because of ...

- the discreet charm of *gossip*?
- or the realistic setting of this social microcosm including current events and the seasonal calendar?
- or the stereotyped mirror image of our pluralist society?
- or the characters, who, as "emotional representatives", incite us to identify with them?
- or the formal structure marked by narrative openness, episodic character, and multiple narrative levels?
- or the fictional communities, which serve as a replacement for traditional family structures which are increasingly breaking down?

In any case the mixture of real life, staged entanglements, personal spleens, and witty punchlines seems to resonate with many teenagers' (and twens') attitudes towards life.

Rationale

Recurring settings, characters and ways of behaviour make understanding foreign language input easier for our learners. The style and register of a sitcom is usually characterized by authentic, idiomatic, conversational English. Sitcoms and soaps also lend themselves as objects of media analysis because "of all moving image media forms, the soap is perhaps the most useful in showing pupils the industrial context of popular media production" (Ib.: 98). What is more important for our students, though, is that they enjoy good comedy, so why not share a good laugh with them? A lot of them watch sitcoms for fun at home, so learning English may become a pragmatic necessity, i.e. to be able to watch one's favourite programme in the original, rather than the dubbed version.

Problems

Understanding sitcoms will remain a challenge, though – at home or at school. Situational humour centred around local particularities and stereotypes, cultural insider information, fast language, puns, or shifting registers make it anything but easy for our learners to follow – and not understanding punchlines means you cannot laugh. So our learners need to be provided with an introduction to the types of humour applied, essential vocabulary, explanations of certain jokes etc..

6.2 Methodology

Selection

Choosing a suitable sitcom or soap very much depends on the personal taste of the teacher – and the learners, of course. Some may favour older British series such as *Fawlty Towers*, *Black Adder*, and *Are You Being Served*, or classic US productions like *The Simpsons*, *Seinfeld*, and *Friends*. More recent ones include the US series *How I Met Your Mother* (set in Manhattan, following the social and romantic lives of five friends, using voice-over narration as a framing device, with the father recounting to his son and his daughter the events that led to his meeting their mother), *Modern Family* (American sitcom centred around three middle-class families living in a 'typical' American neighbourhood, presented in the style of a mockumentary), *The Vicar Of Dibley* (British sitcom featuring Geraldine Grainger as the jolly female vicar of Dibley, a small country village inhabited by 'oddballs'), *Little Britain* (award-accumulating crossover of sketch show and sitcom written and performed by Matt Lucas and David Walliams), or *Come Fly With Me* (mockumentary by Lucas / Walliams, parodying the activities at a fictional airport).

Abb. 4 | Bart Simpson as a giant statue (*The Simpsons*)

Being spoilt for choice, one may resort to awards like "Primetime Emmy Award for Outstanding Comedy Series" and study its winners (below: in bold type) and nominees (www.emmys.com):

Emmys for Comedy Series		
Year	*Program*	*Network*
2011-2012	**Modern Family**	ABC
	30 Rock	NBC
	The Big Bang Theory	CBS
	Curb Your Enthusiasm	HBO
	Girls	HBO
	Veep	HBO
2010-2011	**Modern Family**	ABC
	30 Rock	NBC
	The Big Bang Theory	CBS
	Glee	FOX
	The Office	NBC
	Parks and Recreation	NBC
2009-2010	**Modern Family**	ABC
	30 Rock	NBC
	Curb Your Enthusiasm	HBO
	Glee	FOX
	Nurse Jackie	Showtime
	The Office	NBC
2009	**30 Rock**	NBC
	Entourage	HBO
	Family Guy	FOX
	Flight of the Conchords	HBO
	How I Met Your Mother	CBS
	The Office	NBC
	Weeds	Showtime
2008	**30 Rock**	NBC
	Curb Your Enthusiasm	HBO
	Entourage	HBO
	The Office	NBC
	Two and a Half Men	CBS

Lead-in survey

A more learner-centred way of choosing a sitcom may be to ask all the learners about their favourite sitcom in the form of a class survey.

Class Survey

State your personal opinion of your favourite TV sitcom:

I watch ....

every .... at ....

This sitcom is about ....

....

....

I watch it because ....

....

Genre knowledge

If you also want to increase your learners' film-related knowledge (see ch. 2.2), you can give them a summary of the major features of sitcoms. Whether you hand out the following worksheet and have it filled in in pair work, or use it as a written test for individual work, or start an oral group competition – genre awareness can be raised.

The Genre of Sitcoms

1. A sitcom is a blend word for .... comedy.

2. It is a form of comedy performance originally devised for radio but today typically seen on ... .

3. Sitcoms usually consist of recurring characters, who remain static and unchanging in appearance, for example in the popular animated series The S.................. Other

formats, however, have gradually developed the relationships of the characters (Friends).

4. One or more humorous story lines are centred round a common ...., such as the workplace, a cafe or the family home.

5. A sitcom, in contrast to a soap opera, is usually self-contained, i.e. the events resolve themselves by the end of each episode. Some sitcoms, however, use elements of ongoing storylines such as resorting to an end-of-episode ....-hanger.

6. A typical motif of a sitcom is the .... gag, i.e. a funny remark that characterizes a person and is repeated continually throughout an episode.

7. Traditionally, sitcoms are filmed with a multi-camera setup in front of a live studio ...., then cut and broadcast days or weeks later.

8. Nowadays sitcoms are produced around the globe, and they have become among the most .... programmes on the TV schedule.

9. Many sitcoms are written to run ... minutes in length with commercial breaks, leaving about twenty-four minutes of show-time.

10. Sitcoms are organised in series, which are often sub-divided into .... These may comprise twenty or more episodes.

11. Sitcoms are popular with viewers because they offer attractive characters, funny story-lines, verbal ...., interesting topics, and they structure the viewer's day (week).

12. However, critics accuse them of distorting reality, glorifying the trivial and banal, transporting the wrong values, appealing to .... taste, and seducing viewers into escapism.

Activities

Moving on to actually presenting an example of a sitcom, teachers have to be aware of potential difficulties. Some or even the majority of the learners may know this sitcom inside out, others need to be informed about the setting, main characters (names!), interpersonal relationships – without those basic aspects, understanding is hard. Further activities are summarized in the following table.

Sitcom Activities		
Technique	*Description*	*Tasks*
Episode title	Speculating about the content of the episode	The title of the episode is … . What could it be about?
Title sequence	Orally describing the title sequence (*Vorspann*) guided by questions	1. What's the setting? 2. Who are the characters? 3. Guess at the storyline(s)?
Structure chart	Structuring the film content via a storyboard	Draw a grid (scene number, length, characters, action, time, place) and fill in scene by scene.
Sitcom analysis	Analysing formal features of a sitcom (based on the structure chart)	1. Is it self-contained? 2. Any running gags? 3. What storylines are there? 4. Are they linked? Cuts?
Cinematic analysis	Applying film techniques for studying a selected scene	1. Field sizes? 2. Camera angles? 3. Camera speed, movement? 4. Music, sound and lighting?
Character profile	Describing a person (note-making, individual work)	Choose one of the protagonists and make notes on what he/she does and says. What do you like/dislike?

E & E	English soundtrack – English subtitles	Two scenes: One is watched without, the other with subtitles. Were the subtitles helpful?
E & L1	Cross-lingual analysis: English soundtrack – mother tongue subtitles (via pause button)	One scene: English original is compared with German (French ...) subtitles: translation correct?
L1 & E	Comparing L1 dubbing – English subtitles	German (Spanish ...) dubbing is compared to English subtitles.
Silent subtitles	Reading out the English subtitles with silent viewing mode	Sound off: ... pause button ... dialogue is spoken ... pupils' and actors' speeches are compared.
Extras	Oral or written discussion of DVD bonus materials	Tasks on trailer, music video, cast, interview, audio commentary ...
Review	Stating one's personal opinion on the sitcom	Write a critical review of this episode.
Acting	Role-playing the whole episode / selected scene(s)	Roles distributed ... text learned and rehearsed ... show acted out

A somewhat creative task is to have students design their own sitcom (episode): In groups, guided by a worksheet grid (below), they discuss several dimensions of developing a series, and present their results. An even more challenging and time-consuming extension would be to write a script and film a scene from an episode.

3. Transition: Lots of films are set in New York City, including well-known sitcoms like *How I Met Your Mother*. Let's watch an episode together. But first we have to look at some difficult expressions you need in order to understand: e .g. obsession, insanity, destiny ...
4. Let's meet the main characters in *How I Met Your Mother*: Ted Mosby, Marshall Eriksen, Lily Aldrin, Robin Scherbatsky, and Barney Stinson.

Abb. 7 | Main characters of *How I Met Your Mother*

B. While-viewing (in five parts)
1. First pause after opening sequence (1:35):
   - What do you think about Ted's behaviour? Is he stalking the blonde girl?
   - Is it coincidence that he meets her again in front of the university?
2. Second pause before Barney breaks into Robin's room (5:24):
   - What has happenend so far?
   - Considering how Marshall asked Lily out and Jeanette found Ted, do you think Ted is right that "there is a fine line between love and insanity"?
3. Third pause before "Robin Sparkles 4" (10:45):
   - Why does Barney fly to Canada?
   - Why is Barney so shocked while talking to Robin's ex-boyfriends?
   - What do you think "Robin Sparkles 4 – Underneath the Tunes" may be?

4. Fourth pause after Barney's fight with Alan Thicke (16:01):
   - Robin Sparkles – Underneath the Tunes": real or fake? Why?
   - Why does Robin start to cry in the video after she says "... who doesn't love the mall? Shopping with your friends ..."?
   - What is funny about Robin's music videos? (*P.S. I Love You, Sandcastles in the Sand, In the Mall*)
5. End (21:23):
   - Love is destiny – true? Think of how Lily tried to meet Marshall and how Jeanette followed Ted for 1 ½ years.
   - Recap the episode: Where does love end and obsession begin for you personally? Which of the characters of *HIMYM* is right?

C. Post-viewing (*Homework to be finished within one week:* students choose one out of five tasks)
   1. *Creative Writing:* Imagine the city life of your dreams. Think about place, work, leisure activities, friends etc.
   2. *Graphic Design:* The Mayor of New York City wants you to create an ad poster for young tourists. Design it including information about the most exciting spots plus pictures – make it an eyecatcher!
   3. *Personal Letter:* Is Jeanette a stalker? Why (not)? Should he meet her again? Give him advice in about 200 words. Be prepared to present your pieces of advice in front of your class to one of your fellow students who will pretend to be Ted.
   4. *Factual Analysis:* The sitcom *How I Met Your Mother* repeatedly makes fun of Canada. Compare the US and Canada on a neutral basis, referring to political, economic, cultural, social differences and similarities. Write an essay of about 200 words.
   5. *Film Project:* Produce your own short video of a mockumentary in the style of "Robin Sparkles – Underneath the Tunes". It should be 3-5 min long. Work in groups of 2-3 people at home. You may present your own hometown as if it was New York City that you are talking about. Or you may do a short mock interview of the cast of *HIMYM*, playing the main characters yourselves and talking about what happened in the episode you watched in class.

Sample 2

The following survey lists several techniques and tasks teachers can choose from when working with this episode.

Title	*Friends* (season 1, episode 5): *The One with the East German Laundry Detergent* (script: http://ufwebsite.tripod.com/scripts/105egld.htm)

Length	24 minutes
Synopsis	Joey attempts to make his old girlfriend Angela jealous by tricking Monica into posing as his new girlfriend. Ross tries to start a relationship by teaching Rachel how to do laundry. In order not to snub Janice, Chandler recruits Phoebe to break up with Janice for him.
Topics	Relationships, breaking up and making up, humour, sitcom genre
Level	Upper intermediate – advanced
Time	45 – 90'
Technique	*Friends: Season 1, Episode 5*
Title sequence	1. Describe the setting? 2. What characters are presented? 3. Are there any clues about the storylines?
Structure chart	Draw a grid with seven columns (scene no., length, action, characters, location, time, relevance) and fill them in scene by scene.
Sitcom analysis	1. What storylines can you detect? 2. Are they linked thematically? 3. Describe the cuts between different scenes. 4. Is the end a cliffhanger?
Character profile	Choose one of the six protagonists (Monica, Chandler, Rachel, Ross, Phoebe or Joey) and make notes on how they behave, what they do and say. What do you like / dislike about him / her?
English soundtrack & English subtitles	Scenes 1 and 2 are particularly difficult to understand. Let's watch scene 1 without subtitles, scene 2 with, and summarise the plot in each scene. Are the subtitles helpful for you?
English soundtrack & German subtitles	Scene 7 (launderette): Let's compare the English original with the German subtitles (e.g. "no suds, no save" – "that's not the rule" – "a judgment call"). Is the German translation a good one?
German soundtrack & English subtitles	The German dubbing is compared to the English subtitles, e. g. in scene 6 (Chandler and Phoebe about to break up).
Silent subtitles	Sound off: Every time the pause button is pressed, the dialogue of the subtitles is spoken. Afterwards the pupils' way of speaking is compared to those of the actors / actresses.
Dubbing	Let's watch scene 4 (Ross and Chandler in Ross's apartment) in German (incl. German subtitles). At each turn-taking of the dialogue, the pause button is pressed, and you write down an English translation. Finally read out your English dubbing.

Extras 1: music video	1. The lyrics (www.centralperk-online.de/site/fri/song.htm) are re-written into a nonsense version (e.g. *wife ≠ life*, *a broker ≠ broke*, *niece ≠ knees*), which is handed out and corrected while listening. 2. How, do you think, was this music video produced? 3. Is there any relationship between the lyrics and the content of the episode? 4. Do you like this video?
Extras 2: trailer	1. What did you see? 2. How are the various scenes and images linked? 3. Is this a good trailer? 4. Does it make you want to see the whole film?
Extras 3: cast	1. Choose one actor / actress and take notes on relevant information. 2. Do you think this person is a suitable choice for the role?
Review	Write a critical review of this episode. You may refer to and compare with other (American, Australian, German) sitcoms you know.
Acting	Roles are distributed, the text is learned and rehearsed, and the show is acted out – or: one / several of the 16 scenes (e. g. in the launderette) are acted out.
Filming	Let's script an additional scene and film it.

Tasks

1. Test your knowledge of sitcoms by filling in the Info sheet (6.2.).
2. Take lesson sample no. 2 and choose three tasks you would like to apply in your classroom. Justify your decisions.
3. Choose your favourite sitcom and discuss the pros and cons of using it in a TEFL class.

7 Educational Films

What are *educational films*, do you think? How can they be useful in the EFL classroom?

7.1 Theory

Definition

An *educational film* is a film whose main purpose is to educate and is thus used as an aid in the educational system. Most educational films fall into the broad category of nonfictional motion pictures with a sustained focus on a single topic, presenting facts as well as opinions on this aspect of reality in order to analyse, investigate, express, expose, exhibit, narrate, discuss, reveal, persuade us to have a particular attitude or take some action. They consist of (animated or live) moving pictures, graphics, captions, commentaries, talking heads, interviews, music and sound effects (Aitken 2005, Decke-Cornill 2009, Grimm 2009).

Constructiveness

A feature that scholars emphasise again and again is the constructed character of documentaries. They "... are about real life; they are not real life ... They are portraits of real life, using real life as their raw material, constructed by artists and technicians who make myriad decisions about what story to tell to whom, and for what purpose" (Aufderheide 2007: 2).

Documentaries do not reproduce reality, but construct reality.

The object that is depicted will be manipulated by the filmmaker, who often pursues his/her own agenda and targets a special audience. Consequently documentary discourse oscillates between the concepts of objectivity and subjectivity, fiction and non-fiction, truth and reality (Henseler / Möller / Surkamp 2011: 214).

Types

Thus, there is a variety of mood, tone and style. The following sub-genres of educational films may be distinguished:

- documentaries
- school TV

- classroom films (documentaries adapted in length, difficulty, and topics to the requirements of the classroom)
- hybrid forms (docufiction like *The Buena Vista Social Club*, *Looking for Richard*, docu-soaps, docu-drama, mockumentary = mock documentary etc.)

Abb. 8 | Michael Moore's documentary (?) *Bowling for Columbine*

Structure

In spite of this variety, quite a lot of educational films are structured in a similar essay-like way (Sherman 2003: 62). They often begin with a teaser setting the tone and capturing the attention. Then the subject is introduced in the form of a statement, question or claim, and an overview of the film is given. After that, various sections (similar to paragraphs) support or contradict the claim, seek answers or reveal the truth. The different sections may be linked with pauses, words, images, sounds, music and captions. Serious documentaries give copious references at the end.

History

The following – admittedly rather selective – overview tries to pinpoint a few highlights in the history of documentary und educational film-making (Ellis / McLane 2005):

- 1985: Auguste and Louis Lumière's camera ➤ capturing life around them
- *actuality films* ➤ earliest moving pictures, single-shot unedited clips, length of a minute or less, e. g. a train entering a station
- early 20th century: *travelogue films* ➤ exotic subjects, romantic appeal
- 1922: *Nanook of the North* by Robert Flaherty ➤ first documentary film, showing other cultures
- From 1920s: *newsreel* tradition ➤ re-enactments of events having already happened, e. g. battle footage
- 1926: John Grierson's review of Flaherty's film *Moana* ➤ devising the new use for the word documentary: "the creative treatment of actuality"

- 1920s–1940s: propagandist tradition ➤ persuading an audience of a political conviction, e. g. Leni Riefenstahl's *Triumph of the Will* (1935)
- From the late 1940's on: educational films ➤ produced for classroom use in secondary and tertiary education, 8-mm film cassettes ... DVD, Internet
- 1950s-1970s: *Cinéma vérité* (*Direct cinema*) ➤ authenticity, objective documentary, improvisation with a moving camera, following a person during a crisis, unveiling truth hidden behind superficial reality
- From 1980s: diversification ➤ new hybrid forms (docu-drama, mockumentary etc.)
- 2000s-today: modern documentaries ➤ increasingly successful, far lower budgets than feature films, e. g. *Bowling for Columbine, Super Size Me, Food, Inc., An Inconvenient Truth*
- Today: *reality TV* ➤ events and speech contrived to create an illusion of reality, beginning in 1948: *Candid Camera*, 2000: *Big Brother*

Rationale

Documentaries offer insights into English language target cultures and enable the discussion of political, economic and social issues. They can also contribute to general media literacy: Revealing their constructed character, learners may become informed and critical recipients (Henseler / Möller / Surkamp 2011: 214).

According to Sherman (2003: 62f.), educational films are "highly planned programmes" with a "high focus", the "TV version of a newspaper or magazine article, a kind of essay in words, sound and pictures". Compared to news, they are also topical, but not as ephemeral, slower in pace, the information being less dense, the visual support stronger, though. Documentaries provide access to a vast amount of knowledge and facilitate a sensory encounter with concepts, which actually become an experience to the students (Zane Education 2001). Educational films can also serve as a language model for pronunciation, vocabulary, grammar, and language in its uses and contexts. They usually provide a good mixture of spontaneous and scripted language, the commentator usually speaks in Standard English, at a moderate pace, and with standard phraseology. Interviews offer a linguistic resource of accents and train the comprehension of unscripted spoken language.

Problems

However, educational films usually lack the suspense and glamour of exciting movies. If they provide too much in-depth knowledge, our students will suffer from information overload. As the important message usually lies in the words, viewing may become boring and indigestible. The dialogues are not always easy to understand as they contain exclamations, interjections, overlapping, interruptions, throat-clearing, fillers, and background noises.

7.2 Methodology

Sources

There are educational films about the life of famous or ordinary people, old and new institutions, events and places, history and religion, travel and geography, music and sports, global and local problems, nature and wildlife, art and advertising. The following information may be helpful in the quest for the right material:

- School publishers' brochures: Many of the big publishing houses provide sections with culture videos / DVDs, e. g. *Window on Britain*, which audio-visually answers what British teenagers do during a school day and in their leisure time, or which meals and sports are typical of England.
- Video sellers: A few companies (e. g. Lingua Video, Herbstreuth) have specialized in audio-visual media for language learning purposes. Their range of products covers authors' biographies (from Jane Austen to H.G. Wells), history and politics (M. Moore: *Fahrenheit 9/11*), countries, cities and people (*New Zealand – Island of Adventure*) as well as young learners' films for primary classrooms (*Weather Wise*).
- TEFL drama series: An example of a drama series targeted for EFL learners is *Family Album*, which comprises 26 episodes in two seasons, provides an insight into US everday culture, uses spoken conversational American English, and comes along with course material (teacher's manual with script, annotations and lesson suggestions). Every 25-minute episode consists of three parts, each of which is introduced by a previewing question, and finished by a language focus section (pronunciation, idioms, structures etc.). If your appetite has been whetted, check out an example like episode 4: *A Piece of Cake*

(http://www.youtube.com/watch?v=3hnJyD5WAbE&feature=related).

- School TV (*Schulfernsehen*): Some TV channels have specialized in providing programmes for schools, for example the regional channels in the federal states of Germany. At regular slots during the week, they broadcast (fictional and) non-fictional shows, and offer live-recording service for registered schools (e. g. www.br.de/fernsehen/br-alpha/sendungen/schulfernsehen/faecher/sprachen102.html)
- Websites: Several Internet sites also contain, among others, language sections. A high-quality site, which is often hailed as the best place for language learning of the world, is the "Beeb", which also places British culture clips like *Beyond the Postcard* at your disposal (www.bbc.co.uk/worldservice/learningenglish). Three recommended videos taken from various websites are: *Berlin Etiquette*, an amusing introduction to German everyday customs compared to English-speaking cultures (www.geobeats.com/videos/travel/Germany%20-%20Berlin), *Photo Retouching*, a revealing insight into the step-by-step process of digital photo manipulation (www.youtube.com/watch?v=P4wI_o8gyxA), and *Women, Know Your Limits*, a hilarious spoof on those black-and-white patronising information films of the 1940s – though sexist in political correctness ideology (www.youtube.com/watch?v=P3PwI8jTLK8).
- Educational videoportals: A few online pages are solely dedicated to supplying teachers with instructional films. Two websites which have specialized in docus can be accessed at www.4docs.org and http://documentaryheaven.com. Schulmediathek.tv (www.schulmediathek.tv) is a German site, having more than 1,000 videos in store, for various subjects, ranging in length between one and seven minutes; most of them are in German and English, which may support bilingual teaching. There are also 550 TEFL-specific videos, for example *Proper Pronunciation Currently*. Another example is Planet Schule (www.planet-schule.de), a good website for free quality teaching resources, including free video download of section-divided English educational films, accompanied by description of content and level, background information and worksheets.
- Multimedia CD-ROMs: A famous and award-winning example is *Wizadora*, centred round a young magician of the same

name, who guides her young learners on an adventurous and interactive language trip throughout Great Britain. The whole multimedia box consists of eight ten-minute shows, a CD-ROM and a teacher's manual.
- Videos: A carefully designed, though slightly old-fashioned example is *Snap TV*, which is a documentary culture video, targeted at starter to pre-intermediate students, combining facts, figures and real-life interviews in order to depict the lifestyles of British and American teenagers in their typical domains (free time, music, sport, fashion, school etc.).

Activities

Sherman proposes 40 activities based on educational films (2003: 62ff.). Quite a lot of these ideas seem to be cut out for them, for example *Adopt a character* (➤ recorded interviews with opinionated class members), *Case study* (➤ analysing a social theme), *Daily life* (➤ flow-diagram: information about processes), *Experts* (➤ learning about things), *Famous people* (➤ getting to know personalities), *Maps and journeys* (➤ historical and travelling aspects), *Other people's shoes* (➤ discussing stories about individuals), *Parallels* (➤ comparisons with one's own country), *Vox pop* (➤ round-up of opinions recorded on audio or video).

Critical analysis

As documentaries stage reality, it is important to show how they have been constructed ("... den Konstruktionscharakter von Dokumentarfilmen zu entlarven": Bredella 1994: 87). The following dimensions, which are part of this process of construction, can be analysed with the help of suitable questions (Henseler / Möller / Surkamp 2011: 217ff.).

Analysing Documentaries

Dimension	*Analysis questions / tasks*
1. Defining the genre	• Study various definitions of 'documentary'. • Do they match the docus you have seen?
2. Identifying the perspectives (documentary realism, subjectivity, multi-perspectivity)	• Does this docu reflect reality? • What (multiple) truths are presented? • From what point of view is the docu speaking? • Is there a subjective selection of topics? • How is the film structured? • What is the role of the film-maker? • What strategies are used to suggest authenticity?

3. Identifying the documentary conventions	• What *present techniques* are applied to create a feeling of 'being there'? (unstaged action, improvised dialogue, fly-on-the-wall filming, vox pop, talking head ...) • What *distant techniques* are used to evoke a feeling of 'objectivity'? (expert, voice-over narration, subtitled texts, graphic illustrations, archive material ...)
4. Identifying the modes of reality presentation	• How is reality presented? • Does this docu predominantly follow the observational / expository / reflexive / participatory / performative / poetic mode?
5. Identifying the functions	• What is the purpose of this film? • Is it meant to record / reveal / promote / persuade / analyse / express?
6. Identifying representation	• How are social groups represented? • Who is presenting these groups? • Is the docu voyeuristic?
7. Identifying film techniques	• What do you hear? • How does the music contribute to the presentation of the themes? • Is the voice-over narrator a reliable source of information?

7.3 Lessons

Sample 1

Title	*Teens in South Africa:* *Nandipha between Dancefloor and Township*
Length	10 minutes
Synopsis	Nandipha is a teenage girl living in South Africa. Different situations of her life are presented, for example shopping groceries for a national meal, called Pap, which she also prepares. Furthermore she is shown going to a dance class, solving problems at school and informing others about the risks of AIDS.
Topics	Daily life in South Africa, family, meals, friends, school, AIDS, hopes and future dreams

Level	Medium
Time	45 minutes

Procedure:

A. Pre-viewing
   1. Has anyone ever been to South Africa?
   2. What is the first thing that comes to your mind when you hear 'South Africa'?

B. While-viewing (in three parts: freeze frames)
   1. First freeze frame at 00:00:51: After seeing this short introduction, what, do you think, her living conditions are like?
   2. Second frame at 00:05:20:
      - What sort of life does she live?
      - How does her English sound to you?
   3. End
      - Describe the places you have seen in the video.
      - What impressions did you get from Nandipha?
      - Compare her life with yours.

C. Post-viewing (homework: students choose one out of three options)
   1. *Media transfer:* Write a newspaper article about Nandipha and her daily life.
   2. *Selection:* Choose two situations in the video which surprised you, and explain why you cannot imagine them happening in Britain (or Germany ...).
   3. *Role play:* Write a dialogue between Nandipha and a British pupil going grocery shopping in South Africa, and be prepared to act out this scene (Nandipha explains why they go together, what they can buy there, what dangers they may encounter etc.).

Sample 2

Title	*Teens in South Africa: Michael – Life is Football*
Length	10 minutes
Synopsis	Michael is a boy living in South Africa. He loves playing football and is a ball boy of a team called Santos. He hopes to become a professional football player in the future.
Topics	Daily life in South Africa, football, family, friends, school, hopes and future dreams
Level	Medium
Time	45 minutes (or 90': analysis)

Step	Function	Procedure (6-step approach)
1	Lead-in	• Do you remember where the soccer World Cup 2010 took place? • Can you imagine living in South Africa? • Situation: A South African boy called Michael and his daily life • Viewing purpose: Try to get an insight into Michael's life.
2	First viewing	Presenting the whole video
3	Checking global compre-hension	Tick the correct answers: a) Where does Michael live? ❑ in a big house ❑ in a good neighborhood ❑ in a poor district ❑ in Johannesburg ❑ in Cape Town ❑ in a small house b) What is his favourite meal? ❑ Pasta with meatballs ❑ Fried potatoes ❑ Grilled chicken ❑ Fried bread called roti ❑ Curry ❑ Fish c) What are Michael's free time activities? ❑ Going to the cinema ❑ Playing football ❑ Being with his family ❑ Being a ball boy in a football team ❑ Swimming ❑ Walking in the park
4	Second (guided) viewing	• Focus on the following questions while watching: a) What are the people in Michael's neighborhood like? b) What prevented Michael's father from becoming a national soccer player for South Africa? c) What do you get to know about apartheid? • Presenting the video a 2nd time
5	Checking detailed compre-hension	Discussing the three tasks above in class

6	Follow-up	Elaborating on comprehension: a) Can you identify yourself with Michael? Why (not)? b) Creative writing: Write a letter to Michael, telling him that you have seen the film, what you think about it, and what your daily life is like (your favourite meal, hobbies etc.).
(7)	(Critical analysis)	(Analysing the constructed character of docus: functions, perspectivity, mode of representation, film techniques)

Sample 3

Title	*Family Album* (American TV language course): *A Piece of Cake* (Episode 4) (www.youtube.com/watch?v=3hnJyD5WAbE)
Length	23 minutes 25 seconds
Synopsis	Marilyn, who has just arrived home from her aerobics class, and Richard Stewart, who does weightlifting, argue about which of them is fitter. Richard bets that he can go one hour in his wife's advanced aerobics class and "not feel a thing" – because "it's going to be a piece of cake". ... See who wins the bet ...
Topics	Physical health, fitness craze, aerobics, betting, married life
Level	Intermediate
Time	45'

Procedure:

1. Lead-in
- What do you do to stay healthy?
- Pre-teaching key vocabulary: *aerobics, a bet, exhausted, advanced*
2. Viewing Act I
3. Checking global comprehension: What is the bet? (Who is going to win the bet?)
4. Focus in (language section): Idioms in action (*it's a piece of cake, no sweat, it's tough ...*)
5. Viewing Act II
6. Checking global comprehension: Is Richard in great condition? Say why (not).
7. Focus in (language section): Pronunciation man (reduced vowel sounds: *Waddaya mean?* ...)
8. Viewing Act III

9. Checking global comprehension: Why will they cook dinner together?
10. Focus in (language section): Grammar (*how much* vs *how many*)
11. Evaluation of the film: Did you like it? Why (not)?
12. Homework: Worksheet (Teacher's manual, p. 48: a) how much / how many, b) word search)

Tasks

1. Mention five sources you can access when looking for educational films, and give one example each.
2. Choose one of the three clips and design a 45-minute lesson round it:
   – Berlin Etiquette
   – Photo Retouching
   – Women, Know Your Limits
3. Try to get hold of an episode of *Family Album*. Discuss whether this series is suitable for an intermediate class?

Long Formats

8 Straight Through Approach

Looking back on your school days: When did you watch a movie in class? Did you work on it or just view passively?

8.1 Theory

Definition *Straight through approach* means presenting the whole film en bloc, i.e. without any interruption in one sitting.

Benefits The advantages of this mode are as follows:

- Natural: It is the common way of watching a film, for example when going to the cinema.
- Entertaining: There are no breaks, so suspense is created, and identification with the story or characters is facilitated.
- Simple: Teachers hardly need to do anything other than get hold of the movie and the technical equipment.

Drawbacks The problems, however, are obvious.

The danger of passive consumption looms large as pupils just sit in front of the monitor and watch a film in the same way as they do in their leisure time.

It is a moot question as to whether or how much they actually learn in this mode. If the pupils are not actually focusing, explicit learning does not take place; and the value of implicit learning, i.e. processing complex information in an incidental manner, without awareness of what has been learned, is in dispute. In addition, teachers' professional reputation may be damaged with colleagues (as well as students and their parents) sneering at methods that require no effort at all.

8.2 Methodology

Sources You should have no problems finding a suitable movie. Whether it is one of your personal favourites, or students approach you with an insider tip, whether it is a classical cult movie, or a brand-new Hollywood blockbuster – the choice is huge. To get some orientation in this vast collection of films, you may resort to the Internet Movie Database (www.imdb.com), which claims to be "the biggest, best, most award-winning movie site on the planet". Searches can be guided by titles, names, keywords, characters, quotes, plots, biographies plus further advanced categories. Having found a proper example, you get a (short) plot summary and an (extended) plot synopsis, cast and character information, photos and selected movie clips as well as lots of background details (box office figures, technical specs, trivia, goofs, quotes, FAQs etc.).

Activities

For a change, a film may just be watched for the sake of pure enjoyment, without any activities. The normal case, however, is to frame straight through viewing at least by some (short) introduction (to the topic, plot, setting, characters) and some concluding discussion. The latter may focus on a summary of the story, an evaluation of the quality, or an elaboration of selected issues. The teacher can choose between closed exercises (comprehension questions, true / false statements, gapped summaries, spot the lie texts etc.), and open tasks, from A like "Asking the director" to W like "Wishing you were there" (see chapter 2.3).

Guided movie afternoon (night)

In order to alleviate the general problems posed by straight through viewing (long duration, passive consumption, no learning focus), two variations have turned out to be quite beneficial. One is called *guided movie afternoon (night)* and combines straight through viewing with guidance via tasks (Thaler 2005: 26 – 33). In the first lesson (at school) some introductory background information on the film is given, and observation tasks are distributed to pairs or small groups of students. Each group gets a worksheet, which contains precise tasks, some concise background information on the task, plus space for individual notes. Then the whole class watches the movie in the local cinema; if the town has not got a foreign language cinema, the theatre manager might be persuaded to arrange a one-off screening. The next day the results are discussed in class. The worksheets may be based on the following eight topics:

- Action, story and plot
- Actors, acting and casting
- The male protagonist

- The female protagonist
- Field sizes and editing
- Camera angles, speed and movement
- Sound, lighting and props
- Context, production and message

Blended FBLL

Another technique, which fosters autonomy to an even greater extent, is the combination of classroom teaching and independent film study at home: *blended FBLL* (Doye 1998, Holden 2000). One or more students select a film, watch it at home, and show it in class. For presentation in class, a whole 45-minute lesson may be reserved, in which, after a short introduction and some justification of the selection, a key segment (e. g. exposition) is presented and analysed, before certain aspects are discussed. To make *blended FBLL* as effective as possible, a few requirements must be given:

- Information of students on structure of *blended FBLL*
- Specifications for self-access and classroom phases
- List of suitable films (e. g. Gymnich 2004, Bredella 2004, Grau 2004, Zerweck 2004, Burwitz-Melzer 2004)
- Checklist (guidelines) for film selection
- DVD lending library at school (or multimedia lab for students without technological equipment)
- Teaching a few self-access strategies

Film response journal

As time restrictions do not allow for all members of a class to present their film choices, pragmatic compromises need to be found. One is to recommend film response journals, which are handed in and collected. Teachers should offer a few guidelines on the content and structure (e. g. plot summary, a profile of one protagonist, favourite quotes) and provide language support (e. g. questions, sentence beginnings), but leave enough room for personal reactions (Stempleski / Tomalin 2001: 133). Such individual diaries increase student autonomy even more.

8.3 Lessons

Title	Feature film of your choice
Length	ca. 90'
Synopsis	n.n. (see www.imdb.com)
Topics	n.n.
Level	Intermediate – advanced
Time	180'

Procedure: Blended FBLL

1. Classroom: Introduction to film, group formation (8 groups), explanation of worksheets (one example: see below, Thaler 2005)
   Group 1: Action, story and plot
   Guided by the background information, choose three to five elements of the action, story and plot, and comment on their significance in the film.
   Group 2: Actors, acting and casting
   Guided by the background information, choose three to five aspects related to actors, acting and casting, and comment on their significance in the film.
   Group 3: The male protagonist
   Who is the male protagonist? What does he look like? How does he speak? How is he dressed? How does he behave? What views on life does he represent? What are his relationships with other characters like? Is he likeable? Can you identify with him? Is he a hero? Has a suitable actor been cast for him?
   Group 4: The female protagonist
   Who is the female protagonist? What does she look like? How does she speak? How is she dressed? How does she behave? What views on life does she represent? What are her relationships with other characters like? Is she likeable? Can you identify with her? Is she a heroine? Has a suitable actress been cast for her?
   Group 5: Field sizes and editing
   Guided by the background information, identify three field sizes and two aspects of editing (montage), and comment on their functions in the film.
   Group 6: Camera (see below)
   Group 7: Sound, lighting and props
   Guided by the background information, choose at least one aspect of sound, one of lighting and one of props, and comment on how they contribute to the meaning of the film.
   Group 8: Context, production and message
   Guided by the background information, discuss three to five different aspects referring to the context of production.

2. Cinema (or classroom: double lesson): Watching the film
3. Classroom: Discussing the results (worksheets)
   5 minutes for each group (3' presentation, 2' discussion), final evaluation (5')

Group 6: Camera
Background information: Camera angle refers to the position of the camera in relation to the persons or objects depicted. The most common types are overhead (bird's eye view), eye-level, and below shot (frog's eye view). As a rule, eye-level is neutral und undramatic; overhead reduces the object, making people often seem helpless, weak und humiliated; below shot makes obejcts seem bigger, and thus achieves the opposite – people are made to seem superior, self-confident and powerful. As for camera speed, there is normal motion, slow motion to show a process in more detail, and fast motion. The different types of camera movement are tracking shot (*Fahrt*), pan / panning (*horizontaler Schwenk*), tilt (*vertikaler Schwenk*), and zoom. When the camera moves forward, it penetrates the action and can evoke tension; when it moves backwards, it creates distance from the action, so tension may be reduced, and people seem islolated or lonely. Panning provides the viewer with a feeling of orientation; tilt shows or examines an object in greater detail and can therefore increase tension.
Task: Guided by the background information, identify at least one camera angle, one camera speed, and one camera movement. Comment on their significance in the film.
Notes: ....

Tasks

1. Mention three arguments for and three arguments against the straight through approach.
2. For one of the eight worksheets above (not group 6), write the background information (about 150 words).
3. Suggest a movie you find suitable for the straight through approach, and justify your decision.

9 Segment Approach

Can you imagine showing a movie like *Forrest Gump* in eight parts (lessons)? Say why (not).

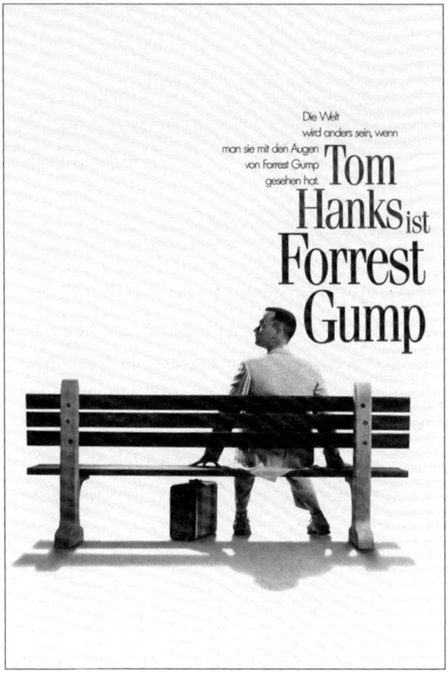

Abb. 9 | *Forrest Gump*

9.1 Theory

Definition

Segment approach means dividing a movie into several segments, which are viewed successively in separate lessons. The individual segments may be of differing lengths, but in practice an average length of approx. 15 minutes seems about right.

Advantages

The benefits of this approach are evident:

- Combining viewing and working: The limited length of the film segments counteracts the danger of passive consumption, leaving enough room for various tasks.
- *Balanced Teaching*: The mixture of receptive and productive activities can strike a fair balance between enjoyment and learning.

- Applying the PWP pattern: Various activities can be used in the pre-, while- and post-viewing phase of each lesson.
- Seeing the entire film: In contrast to the *sandwich approach* (ch. 10) as well as the *clip approach* (ch. 11), students view the whole movie, which allows them to appreciate plot progress and character development.

To conclude, most of the conflicts inherent in FBLL (see ch. 1) can be alleviated by using the segment approach.

The time conflict is solved by using just 15-minute segments, the language conflict can be diminished by including vocabulary work, the reception conflict is reduced by switching on subtitles only in those lessons where they are absolutely needed, and the goals conflict may be overcome by having favourable conditions for Balanced Teaching.

Disadvantages

In spite of this positive conclusion, the problems should not be ignored. The fragmentation of a film often leads to a loss of suspense, impeding a feeling of oblivion, i.e. forgetting about one's problems, immerging into fictitious worlds, being lost to reality. In contrast to straight through viewing, the segment approach represents an unnatural viewing mode, as we usually do not split up a self-contained film into separate pieces. Additionally more classroom time, usually between six and twelve lessons, has to be set apart compared to the sandwich or clip approach (ch. 10 / 11). Finally logistic problems are aggravated as all the technical items required for viewing the film (DVD player or notebook, TV set or projector, loudspeakers, audio cables etc.) need to be provided again and again by the teacher in each of the lessons.

9.2 Methodology

Segmentation

If a lesson lasts 45 minutes, segments of about 15 minutes seem appropriate as they neither present too much nor too little viewing input. Dividing the whole film into separate pieces should, however, not only follow this 15' guideline, but also take thematic coherence and methodological variation into consideration. Tying scenes together which constitute a logical unit is more sensible than slavishly sticking to a rigid time demand.

Variation

With the segment approach, variation as a teaching principle becomes even more important than with the other long formats. The author himself cannot help recalling with pangs of conscience how he applied the same lesson structure for ten consecutive lessons – how boring even an exciting film like *Dead Poets Society* must have become for his learners! To avoid monotony, one can make variations in several areas:

- Length of film segments
- Thematic focus of lessons
- Lesson structure
- Relationship between viewing and discussing
- Balance between the skills and competences targeted
- Closed exercises and open tasks

Beginning

At the beginning of each lesson it is not a bad idea to quickly recap the segment and results of the preceding lesson for the sake of continuity. Instead of asking the same w-questions again and again ("What did we see last time?"), alternatives like oral class chain summaries (every pupil says one sentence), true / false statements, gapped summaries, or lie detector tests (summary contains a few mistakes, which pupils have to identify: "Lie!") present a welcome change from daily routine. An even more student-centred idea may be to delegate the summaries to pupils who take turns presenting the key results of the preceding lesson.

Vocabulary

Some authors also recommend regular vocabulary work to aid viewing comprehension (e. g. Grindhammer 1993). Experience shows that pre-teaching even extended word lists does not guarantee better understanding though, as listening problems result from the peculiarities of spoken English (prosody, intonation, fast and connected speech, slurring, colloquial-conversational style) rather than single phonemes (relevance of chunks!). Two alternatives to traditional, teacher-centred vocabulary work would be to provide dictionaries and make selected 'word experts' look up unknown words when needed (*how to use* ... strategies), or to play *vocab bingo*: students design a bingo sheet with words occurring in the segment to come, crossing it out when heard – and the pupil to have the first row completed wins a small prize.

Viewing options

As the focus in each lesson should vary, teachers can try out numerous viewing procedures. Why not use the bonus tracks on the DVD to look at a certain scene again with the audio commentary by the director to help learners understand the rationale behind it? Or include deleted and extended scenes, which may provide a different image of some of the characters or actions and reveal the constructed nature of film-making? Or switch on and off subtitles in various languages depending on linguistic complexity and learning objectives? Or spontaneously freeze in the frame to study details? Or repeat a dialogue that has turned out to be too difficult to understand?

Lit and cin

Finally, literature and cinematography seem to be good companions for the segment approach. The short duration of the segment leaves teachers sufficient time to compare a written piece of literature with the corresponding audiovisual adaptation (see ch. 12). For the same reason, and for the sake of variation, a one-lesson focus on film analysis should be included.

9.3 Lessons

One film – three approaches: The cult movie *Dead Poets Society* can be dealt with in various ways.

Abb. 10 | The final scene of *Dead Poets Society*

Sample 1 (Thaler 2003)

This teaching material consists of five components, which are based on six didactic premises: dealing with the film and not the book, varying methods and techniques, setting content before form, limiting the amount of time set apart for the project, focusing on obvious key aspects, and complementing closed teaching by integrating open methods.

Title	*Dead Poets Society* (DVD: Touchstone Home Entertainment, 2002, No. 100947)
Length	128 minutes
Synopsis	This American drama directed by Peter Weir and starring Robin Williams (1989) is set at the conservative Welton Academy in Vermont in 1959. It tells the story of Mr Keating, an English teacher who inspires his students (Neil Perry, Todd Anderson, Knox Overstreet, Charlie Dalton, Richard Cameron, Steven Meeks, and Gerard Pitts) through his teaching of poetry. In contrast to the ethos of the elite prep school ("tradition, honor, discipline and excellence"), Keating uses unorthodox teaching methods, whistling the 1812 overture and taking them out of the classroom to focus on the idea of carpe diem ...
Topics	Education, (boarding) school, ways of living, human responsibility, integrity, self-fulfillment, idealism vs. realism, conformity vs individuality, poetry
Level	Advanced
Time	Between 8 (without poetry workshop and post-viewing activities), 12 (reduced post-viewing phase) or 15 lessons

Procedure:

Component 1
Setting & protagonists (intensive viewing)
1st lesson: setting (DVD chapter 1)
➤ viewing-listening, speaking, board sketch
2nd lesson: cinematography (ch. 2)
➤ viewing, cinematographic devices, worksheet 1
3rd lesson: Keating's Pritchard poetry lesson (10 minutes)
➤ viewing, teacher's philosophy, board sketch
4th lesson: first cave meeting (9 minutes)
➤ viewing, group work, poetry

Component 2
Dead & living poets (stopover: poetry workshop)
5th lesson: dead poets come alive
➤ station learning (5 stations), reading, evaluating, poetry, worksheets 2-6
6th lesson: classroom cave (room darkened)
➤ writing, enjoying, discussion

Component 3
Keating's followers & antagonists (extensive viewing)
7th lesson: movie time (DVD chapters 5-8, 40 minutes)
➤ guided viewing, worksheets 7-11
8th lesson: jigsaw time
➤ discussion, group work, jigsaw approach

Component 4
Climax & finale
9th lesson: Neil's suicide (ch. 9, 18')
➤ viewing, symbolism, atmosphere, worksheet 12
10th lesson: Oh Captain, my Captain! (last chapter, 17')
➤ viewing, evaluation

Component 5
After & beyond
11th-12th (or 15th) lessons: free work (*Freiarbeit*)
➤ material guided work, worksheets 13-24
➤ presentations, discussion, evaluation

Sample 2 (Liebelt 1995)

Wolf Liebelt's scene index contains 98 scenes. Each of them consists of a short description of the situation and a few questions as well as indications of length scene and counter time (DVD player). The teacher's manual suggests answers for all the questions. The following excerpt covers the first five scenes.

Dead Poets Society (Liebelt 1995)			
Scene / Question	Questions	Length	Counter
Scene 1	Chapel of Welton Academy: Introductory scenes. Film credits. Last preparations for opening ceremony.	2,05	0:00:00
Q1	Name the mini-scenes at the beginning of the film before Headmaster Nolan makes his speech.		
Q2	What is the function of these numerous short scenes/glimpses?		
Q3	What impression do we get of the school, the parents, teachers and students?		
Q4	In which order does the procession enter the chapel?		
Scene 2	Headmaster Nolan's speech with introduction of Keating.	1,53	0:02:05
Q1	Characterize Nolan based on his facial expression and on the way he talks.		
Q2	Name the "four pillars" of Welton Academy.		
Scene 3	Outside: Parents say good-bye to their sons.	1,44	0:03:58
Q1	What does Nolan say to Todd?		
Q2	What does Nolan say to Neil?		
Scene 4	Neil and other boys in Neil's room.	1,30	0:05:42
Q1	Name the "four-pillar-version" of the boys.		
Scene 5	Mr. Perry in Neil's room: Argument about too many extracurricular activities.	1,51	0:07:12
Q1	How does Neil address his father?		
Q2	What does this form of address reveal about the father-son relationship?		
....	....	....	....
Scene 98	....	....	....

Sample 3 (Grindhammer 1993)

Lucille Grindhammer has divided the movie into eight ca. 15-minute segments, each segment being the basis of a 45-minute classroom period. She aims at fostering the basic language skills (speaking, listening, reading, writing), while introducing students to an analytical but not an academic approach to a popular Hollywood movie. While preparing her teaching sequence, she identified difficult vocabulary, decided on the kind of language skill she wanted to expand, considered the issue which should be focused on (content or film technique oriented), developed a suitable exercise, and envisioned formats for the students to work out those exercises. Thus her eight segments follow this structure:

- Pre-viewing: Before showing the segment, teachers can go through a list of difficult words, and read through the questions / tasks which form the basis of the following discussion.
- Viewing: The 15-minute segment is watched.
- Post-viewing: The points are discussed together, and details which students recall are collected.
- Homework: Each lesson ends with some assignments.

Tasks

1. Point out three advantages and three problems of the segment approach.
2. Turn to the movie *Dead Poets Society* and do one of the two tasks.
   a) Watch chapter 1 (DVD Touchstone Home Entertainment, 2002, No. 100947) and design a board sketch focusing on setting and protagonists.
   b) Guided by the following scene survey, watch chapter 2, focus on cinematography, and answer the five questions:

Scene no.	*Contents*	*Time (min. sec.)*
1	Countryside with ducks	00.00
2	Boys on the staircase	00.17
3	Chemistry, Latin and trigonometry classes	00.35
4	Keating's *Carpe Diem lesson*	00.47
5	Students leaving class	06.35
6	Boys in the showers	06.59
7	Todd in his room	07.29
8	Dr Hager and Knox on their way to the Danburrys	07.56
9	Knox at the Danburrys	08.37
10	Radio experiment in the study hall	09.26 – 10.47

1. Symbolism
What is the function of the birds in scene 1?
2. Directing Sympathy
Why do the glimpses at chemistry, Latin and trigonometry classes precede Keating's first English lesson?
3. Atmosphere
What atmosphere is created in the Honor Room (scene 4)? How and why is this done?
4. Montage
How are scenes 6 and 7 linked?
5. Foreshadowing
How does scene 8 foreshadow the ninth scene?

3. Choose one of the three approaches to *Dead Poets Society* (Grindhammer, Liebelt, Thaler) and evaluate its benefits and drawbacks.

10 Sandwich Approach

Do you mind watching just parts of a film rather than the whole film? Say why (not).

10.1 Theory

Sandwich approach means showing only parts of a film, not the whole film. As in a sandwich, scenes which are viewed alternate with scenes that are omitted. Definition

The advantages of this approach are evident: Benefits

- Viewing and working: Like the segment approach, it allows a lesson to be split up into viewing parts and stages where the selected sequence is discussed.
- PWP: The film excerpts can be exploited by setting activities before, during and after the viewing.
- Gain in time: Compared to the segment approach, less classroom time needs to be spent.
- Setting priorities: Irrelevant or undesirable scenes can be skipped, and key sequences are emphasized.

Despite these positive points a few problems linger on. As with the segment approach, the level of film appreciation suffers when it is divided into digestable portions. The fact that the complete movie is not shown may result in distorted perception and lack of understanding – viewers do not get the whole picture. Furthermore more classroom time has to be invested in comparison to the clip approach (ch. 11). Drawbacks

10.2 Methodology

A sandwich consists of various layers. There must be at least two slices of film, and more substantial teaching sequences will comprise three, four and more pieces of audiovisual foundation. The fillings between them are supplied by well-assorted tasks and exercises. A variety of savoury discussion points and spicy homework assignments is likely to refine the taste of this dish. The Varieties bread – sorry, the film – can be used as it is, or may be seasoned with subtitling or fast forward to enhance flavour and texture.

The most frequent reason to resort to the sandwich approach is usually the wish to save time because you do not need to show the whole film.

Skipping

The question as to which parts should be skipped may lead to these omissions:

- Insignificant scenes: Dispensable sequences are those that do not advance the plot, reveal no further characteristics of the protagonists, or contribute little to the meaning of the film.
- Boring scenes: In nearly any movie, you are certain to find parts that are not as thrilling as others.
- Unfeasible scenes: From a TEFL point of view, parts with no language input or linguistically controversial speech may lack in learning potential.
- Taboo scenes: The teachers in their role as educators have to decide how much violence, sexuality, sexism, tackiness or profanity they can expect their teenagers to endure.

Compensations

Although those scenes are omitted, it does not necessarily mean that they are completely ignored. To secure understanding, the skipped parts may be supplemented by oral (or / and) written form – telling (writing) instead of showing. To make up for the omissions, various types of activities can be made use of:

- Questions ➤ *intelligent guessing*
- True / false statements
- Oral and written summaries
- Gapped summaries
- Spot the lie texts
- Scene index (showing the list of scenes via transparency and pointing to the omissions)
- Film experts (students taking turns at watching the skipped scenes at home and summarizing the content orally in class during the next lesson)

As the major argument for adopting the sandwich approach is to save time, these activities should not take too long. A final option of dealing with skipped scenes is to bluntly tell the learners that they are not relevant or appropriate.

10.3 Lessons

Abb. 11 | Finale of *Monty Python's Life of Brian*

Title	*Monty Python's Life of Brian*
Length	94 minutes
Synopsis	The movie tells the story of Brian Cohen, a young Jewish man who is mistaken for the Messiah because he was born on the same day as Jesus Christ, and next door to him. This 1979 British comedy film, which was written, directed and largely performed by the Monty Python comedy team, triggered a highly controversial discussion at the time of its release. Since then, it has often been hailed as the "greatest comedy film of all time" by several newspapers (The Guardian, 2007), magazines and TV networks.

Topics	Religious satire (belief in miracles, intolerance), (accusations of) blasphemy, political satire (poking fun at revolutionary groups and 1970s British left-wing politics), mass hysteria, individuality vs herd instinct, comedy / farce
Level	Advanced
Time	5 lessons of 45' each

Procedure (Thaler 2000):

Lesson I:
The Opening: Brian and Jesus (first 13 minutes of film, 4 scenes)
➤ lead-in (anagram: FIRE NOBLE FAITH ... The Life of Brian), guided viewing, three groups (opening credits, Jesus preaches, the stoning), worksheet, genre of *parody*, homework

Omission I: 4 minutes, scenes 5/6, content: The ex-leper, Mandy tells Brian he is a Roman

Lesson II:
Political Background: Roman Oppression vs Judean Independence (film: 8')
➤ 5 questions to summarize the omissions (worksheet: below), viewing scene 7 (Brian meets the PFJ at the forum, 5') twice, summarizing content on the board, viewing scene 8 (Romanes Eunt Domus, 3') once, comprehension questions, homework

Omission II: 25', scenes 9-15, content: The commandos, The raid on Pilate's palace, The ancient prisoner, Pontius Pilate, Brian and the spaceship, haggler Harry, Guards search Matthias's house

Lesson III
The New Messiah: Brian Superstar (scenes 16-19, 17')
➤ 10 true / false statements to summarize and make up for the omissions (worksheet: below), pre-teaching key vocabulary, guided viewing (worksheet: below), double viewing of key scene, homework

No omission

Lesson IV
Pontius Pilate: Language "Pwoblems" (scenes 20-23, 7')
➤ viewing comprehension, comparing English original with German dubbing (How are Pilate's language problems translated into another language?), reading out Pilate's speech (worksheet), analyzing parody on English character traits (boardsketch), homework

Omission III: 6', scenes 24-30, content: The jailer and his assistant, Bigguth' thpeech, Crucifixion party, Pilate gives the crowd one more chance, Parvus and Mr Cheeky, The centurion questions the jailer, The PFJ leaves

Lesson V:
Finale: The Crucifixion (last scene, 3')
➤ gapped summary to make up for the omissions (worksheet: below), double listening-viewing of final song *Always Look on the Bright Side of Life*, discussing song, correcting a mondegreen version of the song, final evaluation of the whole movie, optional: transfer activities

Skipping Deleted Scenes, I: Questions

Each point consists of a statement and a question. Try to answer the questions by *intelligent guessing* (an *educated guess*).

1. Brian and Mandy meet an ex-leper. Who cured him?
2. The ex-leper pursues Brian and Mandy relentlessly through the streets. Why?
3. He is not happy that he has been cured by Jesus. Why not?
4. Mandy tells Brian that his father was not a Jew. What nationality could he have been?
5. Brian learns that he is a Roman. How does he react?

Skipping Deleted Scenes, II: True / False

As a summary of the first 15 scenes, 10 true / false statements are read out. The last four refer to the deleted scenes 9 – 15.

1. Brian was born two thousand years ago, on the same day as Jesus Christ.
2. The four Magi brought gifts and hailed Brian as the new Messiah everywhere.
3. After Brian had heard Jesus preach, he went to the hanging of a man, who was accused of stealing.
4. Brian earned his living by selling popcorn in the streets of Judea.
5. When Brian was 43 he joined the Judean Popular Front.
6. Caught writing an anti-Roman slogan on the city walls Brian was ordered by Roman soldiers to write the correct slogan 100 times all over the walls.
7. The PFJ planned to raid Pilate's palace and take his wife as a hostage.
8. While they were making their way to Brian's wife, they met another revolutionary group and started partying with them.
9. Brian was caught by Roman soldiers and taken to Pontius Pilate, but managed to escape with the help of an alien spaceship.
10. After that he hid on a balcony, which suddenly collapsed.

Skipping Deleted Scenes III: Gapped Summary

Complete the gaps in this summary of scenes 24 – 30 by using the words below.

As the Romans do not have a Roger or Roderick in their prisons, Pilate finally decides to .... (1) Brian. However, through a .... (2), the soldiers take Mr Cheeky off the cross, who was only .... (3) their legs when .... (4) to be Brian. Brian is nailed to the cross, but then he sees the .... (5) approaching. Reg reads out a satement on behalf of the movement, they sing "For he's a .... (6) good fellow" and leave him. After the PFJ Otto's army arrives and all its members commit .... (7). Judy rushes up, thanks Brian for his .... (8) behaviour and hastens off. Mandy is of no help either because she just .... (9) him of only thinking of sex. Brian is utterly depressed, but the man from the cross behind attempts to .... (10) him up.

Words: terrific – misunderstanding – release – accuses – revolutionaries – pulling – jolly – pretending – cheer – suicide

Brian Superstar

1. **Pre-viewing: *Vocabulary work***

Match the words on the left with the definitions on the right.

gourd	s.o. who does not believe what is generally accepted
lilies	evergreen shrub with dark berries (*Wacholder*)
vow	having no hair on the scalp
heretic	hard-skinned fleshy fruit of a climbing plant
juniper	a plant growing from a bulb
bald	a solemn promise

2. **Viewing Scenes 16-18: *Comprehension***

2.1 What does Brian preach?
2.2 How do the people react?
2.3 Why is Simon angry about Brian?
2.4 What do Brian's followers intend to do with Simon and why?

3. First viewing of Scene 19: Finish the statements.

3.1 Mandy insults Judith because .....

3.2 Judith explains the presence of the crowd outside by claiming .....

3.3 Brian tells the crowd that .....

4. Second viewing of Scene 19

4.1 *Listening comprehension*: Fill in the gaps in Brian's speech:

"Look, you've got it all wrong. You don't need to .... me. You don't need to follow .... You've got to think for .... You're all ...."

"You're all ...."

"Well, that's it. You've all got to .... it ...... for yourselves."

4.2 *Analysis*: How would you interpret the crowd's reaction?

5. Analysis: *Satirical intention*

The following passages occur in scenes 16-19. What may have Monty Python intended to criticize? Can you find parallels in modern society? Talk in pairs first, make notes, and then share your ideas with the rest of the class.

"Don't pass judgement on other people, or you might get judged yourself." (Brian)

....

In no time, Brian has a crowd of fanatic followers, worshipping his gourd and shoe.

....

The crowd believes Brian has worked some miracles (juniper bush, blind man).

....

They want to kill Simon because he does not believe in Brian.

....

Brian – Judith – Mandy – crowd

....

"Yes, we're all individuals." "Yes, we are all different." (The crowd)

....

Tasks

1. Point out three arguments for and three against the sandwich approach.
2. Watch *Monty Python's The Life of Brian* – without the scenes skipped – and do one of the following tasks:
   a) Answer the three worksheets on deleted scenes (see above).
   b) Complete the worksheet on "Brian Superstar".
3. Take a movie you would like to work with in class and sketch a sandwich approach to it: First decide on four to six lessons with a topical focus each, then choose scenes to be skipped and justify your deletions, finally design one exercise for dealing with skipped scenes.

11 Clip Approach

Try to remember a film scene which you like very much. How could it be used in an English lesson? Why?

11.1 Theory

Clip approach means presenting only one part of a film. This single piece can be one scene or a sequence of several scenes, and the length of the clip may vary between a few seconds and ten or even more minutes. Definition

The benefits of this approach are obvious: Advantages

- Focus: Teachers can select a key scene and draw their learners' attention to the particular details in this excerpt.
- Time: Of the four major approaches to long formats, the clip approach takes up least classroom time, so the argument about time pressure due to demanding syllabuses does not apply here.
- Flexibility: Owing to their brevity and variety, clips offer infinite possibilities for teaching. They can serve numerous learning objectives and be adjusted to specific needs.
- Activation: The risk of passive viewing is very low. Films that otherwise might be assessed by learners as boring, too long, too slow or too old, appear acceptable in a slimmed down version.
- Authentic alternative: It is true that by now contemporary textbooks are often accompanied by scripted audiovisual materials, which are useful to expose learners to particular linguistic aspects (grammatical structures, lexical phrases) in spoken communicative situations. The problem, however, is that in terms of clarity, technical standards and artistic value, those instructional clips cannot compete with compelling feature films. What we see in movies is not real, "the language spoken in film is often performed text, but it is a performance where native speakers suspend disbelief and accept the dialogue as 'real'" (Kaiser 2011: 233). Kaiser also reminds us that "film is concerned with and portrays the burning social, economic, and political issues of the day, as well as peoples' reac-

tions to these issues" (Ibid.) – and well selected clips can make learners reflect on these issues.
- Pedagogy: Non-appropriate content of a film can be excluded.
- Extramural English: If their appetite has been whetted, learners may be induced to watch the whole movie outside the classroom.

Drawbacks

The last two points, however, already imply some of the problems when using the clip approach. Teachers could be blamed for learners watching the rest of the film, which may include inappropriate content, out of class – with parents possibly complaining about it. Moreover singling out one scene means taking it out of its context, which is likely to distort its overall meaning. Related aspects that contribute to a full understanding and appreciation of a film are ignored. In addition, watching just a McDonaldized film nugget will not transport viewers into a state of delightful entertainment and thrilling suspense.

11.2 Methodology

Selection

Basically there are two ways to choose a proper clip: Either you happen to be fascinated by a film scene and start musing about how to exploit it in class (material-driven approach), or you start from the learning objective and look for a suitable clip (goal-driven approach). The latter, in particular, is likely to turn out as a rather time-consuming enterprise. It helps, of course, if teachers are film aficionados, have seen quite a number of films, make notes of potentially useful scenes, ask different people for suggestions, or browse the web.

A part of the film that generally lends itself to rich exploitation is its opening.

Exposition

The movie exposition, as in a literary piece, is very important as it sets the scene, introduces the main characters, sets the mood, hints at the theme, raises suspense, and gets the story going. Whether the opening scene appears chronologically at the beginning of the story, or starts in the middle of the plot (in medias res), or first depicts the end of the story, telling the plot backwards (Hecke 2010) – the first scenes usually contain the highest density of information.

Variety

As a matter of fact, which scene you pick primarily depends on what you want to achieve. It may introduce a short warm-up activity or extend to a big project, it can motivate learners to speak or write, it may trigger a role play for beginners or a film review for advanced students, it may focus our attention on characters or plot, it can be used for language practice or philosophical debates, it serves verbal or non-verbal parameters (body language). The brevity of the format makes it suitable for repeated viewing, freeze-frame based description, intensive analysis, and cross-lingual comparisons (via subtitles). An appropriate set of pre-, while-, and post-viewing activities will target both at the linguistic difficulties and the thematic contextualization of the clip. The range of use is huge, as Sherman (2003) makes clear:

Range of Using Clips

Focus	*Examples*
Language domains	Grammatical structures, vocabulary, idioms, expressions, pronunciation, intonation etc.
Speech functions	Applying for a job, inviting so., ordering sth. in a restaurant, phoning a friend, bargaining etc.
Native and non-native speaker accents	UK (north and south), US (north and south), Indian, Scottish, Irish, Canadian, Australian etc.
Common settings	Airport, pub, train, school, family home, sports club, holiday resort etc.
Arrays of common objects	The content of a First Aid box, a dinner table, a teenager's room etc.
Body language and facial expressions	In a job interview, when strong emotional feelings are displayed etc.

Activities

Why not try out some of the numerous suggestions by Sherman (2003) and Stempleski / Tomalin (2001):

- *What's it all about?* Based on a still from a clip, students (from elementary level) create a script. The teacher chooses a dramatic scene with two characters, writes down a few questions on the board (*What's the situation? Who are these people?*

Where are they? What are they doing? What are they talking about?), divides the class into pairs, shows the freeze-frame, and asks students to analyze it by discussing the questions above. Possible storylines are suggested, some of which are presented in front of the class. In a follow-up task the pairs can write a one-minute script based on their ideas and act it out.

- *Wordhunt*: A clip can also be used for teaching grammatical structures such as tenses, definite articles and the verb *to be*. The learners search structures, write them down, count them, and repeat the grammatical feature. It is hoped that structures will be memorized more easily when grammar is linked to authentic film. This task can be aided by a transcript and some gap-fill exercises.
- *Hidden Meanings*: You need a short clip in which the figures experience emotional depth, but are not able to express it in words. First the term *subtext* is explained, then the clip is shown twice (with pauses or freeze frames if necessary), and the students try to read between the lines. To scaffold learners' speculations, questions (*Did the character mean what he / she said? If not, what did he / she mean? What does character X think about what character Y said?)* and a list of sentence starters (*It's possible, but ..., He / she might be wondering whether ...*) can be provided. In a post-viewing activity a letter, in which the character describes his / her feelings and thoughts to a friend, could be written.
- *Cinematic grid*: The clip approach is the one for cinematic devices par excellence. As observing, describing and analyzing the various techniques is quite a challenging task, dividing the work between several groups and providing them with clear instructions as well as suitable phrases in the form of a grid or table has proven to be a helpful idea.
- *Listen to the music*: The fact that music plays an important though often neglected part in film analysis can be demonstrated by watching a film without sound or swapping the music from sad to happy. Film music serves numerous functions, for example to arouse the viewer's attention, evoke feelings, create atmosphere, intensify visual impressions, or contradict the pictures (Lütge 2012: 71ff.). To introduce learners to the relevance of film music, two clips with atmospheric

music are chosen. First the teacher introduces different film genres (thriller, romance, western etc.), then pairs of students listen to the first clip without seeing the visuals, and have to predict the genre. The same procedure takes place for the second clip, and the ideas are collected on the board. Eventually both clips are played with vision and sound, and the solutions are compared with the students' previous predictions.

11.3 Lessons

Sample 1

Title	*Forrest Gump*: opening credits, first scene (00:00 – 4:30)
Length	4:30 minutes
Synopsis	This extremely popular and award-winning Robert Zemeckis film, adapted from a Winston Groom novel, follows the life of low-I.Q. Forrest Gump (Tom Hanks) and his meeting with Jenny, the love of his life. It chronicles Forrest's accidental experiences with some important people and events in America from the late 1950's to the 1970's, e. g. he meets with Elvis Presley, John F. Kennedy and Richard Nixon, and he fights in Vietnam, takes part in a peace rally and sets up Apple company. At the outset of the film, we see a feather drifting randomly in space above Forrest, and then landing at Forrest's feet. The protagonist picks it up and starts telling the story of his life to people accidentally sitting next to him at the bus stop – "... Life is like a box of chocolates; you never know what you're going to get."
Topics	Opening scene: functions of film beginnings, symbolism (feather, box of chocolates), cinematic techniques
Level	Intermediate – advanced
Time	45 minutes

Procedure:

Pre-viewing
Activating background knowledge on the film

While-viewing
1. First viewing (sound off)
   Guiding task: What happens?
2. Checking comprehension

3. Second viewing (with sound)
   A worksheet (see below) is handed out, six groups are formed, each group has to focus on one of the six tasks and fill in the worksheet.
4. Presenting and discussing the results

Post-viewing
Conclusion: What functions does the opening scene serve?

***Forrest Gump*: Opening Scene (Exposition)**	
Group 1: setting Focus on the time and place of the scene.	
Group 2: suspense How is suspense created? Look at the people and objects.	
Group 3: protagonist Observe his appearance, way of communication, and body language.	
Group 4: symbolism What may the feather, worn-out shoes, suitcase, and box of chocolates signify?	
Group 5: camera What camera shots can you identify? Why? How does the camera move?	
Group 6: sound Listen to the film score and background sounds. Describe them. What might they express?	

Sample 2

Abb. 12 | Billy Elliot does ballet

Title	*Billy Elliot* (24:40-27:15, Universal-DVD: Billy Elliot – I Will Dance, or: http://movieclips.com/2X9E-billy-elliot-movie-not-for-lads, or: www.youtube.com/watch?v=jmgV3OFnoaE)
Length	2:30 minutes
Synopsis	Eleven-year-old Billy Elliot grows up in the North of England during the 1980's. His widowed father, a hard working and underpaid mine worker, wants Billy to take weekly boxing lessons. The young boy, however, soon finds out that his passion is ballet. When his dad learns about his secret hobby, he asks Billy to quit his dancing classes.
Topics	Father-son relationship, gender roles, homosexuality, (sexual) stereotyping, teenage lives
Level	Intermediate
Time	45 minutes

Procedure:

A. Pre-viewing

1. What, in your opinion, are typical male and female sports?
2. Vocabulary: Match the new words with the right meaning.

lads	'damn'
Aye	'grandma'
hiding	a classical dance form
frigging	(pejorative) homosexual person
ballet	'yes'
Nana	a 'beating'
poof	(coll.) 'boys'

B. While-viewing

1. First viewing: vision only (sound off)
Observation task: What different kinds of emotions can you observe?
2. Checking the observation task
3. Second viewing (normal viewing, sound on)
Task: Fill in the gaps of Billy´s and Dad´s conversation (*simple gap-fill*).

Billy: What´s wrong with ....?

Dad: What´s .... with ballet?

Billy: It´s perfectly ....!

Dad: .... normal?

Grandma: I used to go to ballet.

Billy. See?

Dad: Aye for your nana. For ...., not for lads, Billy. .... do ....

or .... or wrestling. Not friggin' ballet!

4. Checking gap-fill

C. Post-viewing

1. What does Billy´s Dad mean by saying 'You perfectly know what's wrong with ballet!'? How do you feel about this accusation?
2. *(beforehand: giving the students some background information about the social circumstances and the mine workers' strikes during the 1980's)* What may be the reason why Billy's Dad wants his son to learn boxing? Why is he disappointed when he finds out about his son's hobby?

3. Creative Writing (homework): Choose one of the following tasks.
   - Imagine you were Billy. Write a diary entry about your Dad's reaction and how you feel about it.
   - Imagine you were Billy. Write a letter to your best friend. Explain what happened and tell him whether you are continuing with ballet dancing or not.

Tasks

1. Name three advantages and three disadvantages of using the clip approach.
2. Watch the opening scene of *Forrest Gump* and fill in the worksheet.
3. Have a look at the *Billy Elliot* clip and the lesson about it. Discuss the value of *silent viewing*, i.e. showing a clip without sound.

Special Formats

12 Film Adaptations

- What book have you read recently? Could you transform it into a film?
- What is difficult about putting text into film?
- How can you express internal action (feelings, thoughts) in a film?
- Is it justified to compare book and film? State your opinion.

12.1 Theory

Definition

The term *film adaptation* refers to the transformation of a written work, in whole or in part, into a film (McFarlane 1996, Stam 2005, Surkamp 2009). This type of transformation usually involves elisions and interpolations, and has been a ubiquitous practice of film-making from the earliest days of cinema (Branigan 1992, Cartmell 2012, Hutcheon 2006). "Since the beginning of cinema, adaptations have been a staple of the business of film. Among the earliest films were adaptations of literary works" (Cartmell 2012: 2). And this trend has continued: "Film-makers' reasons for this continuing phenomenon [of ransacking literature for source material] appear to move between the poles of crass commercialism and high-minded respect for literary works" (McFarlane 1996: 7). Whatever the main reason is – adaptations are everywhere today. A literary source can also be transferred to other genres or media such as a stage play or even a video game, which is called *literary adaptation*.

Forms

A widespread type of film adaptation is using a novel as the basis of a feature film. Yet other works of fiction – and non-fiction – can also be adapted into short or feature length films. Often plays are used as sources, and William Shakespeare might be called the most popular screenwriter in Hollywood. The following table lists the most important sources with some examples favoured in TEFL classrooms:

Forms of Film Adaptations	
Genre	*Examples*
Novel	• Nick Hornby: *About a Boy* ➤ Chris / Paul Weitz: *About a Boy* (2002) • Doris Pilkington: *Follow the Rabbit-Proof Fence* ➤ Phillip Noyce: *Rabbit-Proof Fence* (2002) • Virginia Woolf / Michael Cunningham: *Mrs Dalloway / The Hours* ➤ Stephen Daldry: *The Hours* (2002)
Play	• Willy Russell: *Educating Rita* ➤ Lewis Gilbert: *Educating Rita* (1983) • Arthur Miller: *Death of a Salesman* ➤ Volker Schlöndorff: *Death of a Salesman* (1985) • Oscar Wilde: *The Importance of Being Earnest* ➤ Oliver Parker: *The Importance of Being Earnest* (2002)
Short story	• E.A. Poe: *Tell-Tale Heart* ➤ animated version, 1953: www.youtube.com/watch?v=W4s9V8aQu4c • Annie Proulx: *Brokeback Mountain* (1997) ➤ Ang Lee: *Brokeback Mountain* (2005)
Poem	• Rudyard Kipling: *If* • Tim Burton: *Vincent* (www.youtube.com/watch?v=hD8uQzuolLo)
Comic book	*Superman*
Radio narrative	*The Hitchhiker's Guide to the Galaxy*
Picture book	Maurice Sendak: *Where the Wild Things Are* (www.youtube.com/watch?v=6cOEFnppm_A)

Faithfulness

When comparing book and film, the question of *faithfulness* inevitably arises. Critics of adaptations argue that the film must be accurate at least to the effect, the theme or the message of the book – and the more high profile the source book, the more imperative the demands of accuracy. However, change in adaptation is inevitable, required both by the constraints of time and the peculiarities of the medium.

Furthermore a comparison must not be guided by a prejudiced preference for the written word, denigrating the audiovisual version as an inferior product. Book and film are two different media with their own aesthetic forms and functions. A novel is a novel, while a movie is a movie – both are works of art, which must be seen as separate entities (Giddings / Selby / Wensley 1990, Leitch 2012, McFarlane 1996).

Kreuzer's distinction

As to the question of fidelity, Kreuzer (1993) proposes four subdivisions of adaptations:

- Appropriation of literary material: a rather indirect type of adaptation, which only borrows some elements (e. g. certain motifs or characters)
- Illustration: trying to keep as many elements (story, plot, dialogue) from its literary source as possible, attempting a one-to-one translation to the screen, largely ignoring the particularities of the different media
- Transformation: aiming at a work of art that is analogous to the literary text (its meaning or spirit), but making use of specifically cinematic ways of narration and representation
- Documentation: filming a theatre performance

There are some more classifications, e. g. Wagner's three categories (1975: 22, *transposition*, *commentary*, and the slightly confusing term of *analogy*), or Poppe's five types (2007), which do not really add more value to related classroom work.

Rationale

Apart from the arguments which speak for using literature and using films in general, Lütge (2012: 76) mentions two further points. Teachers and learners view variety in the classroom as enriching; the mere prospect of watching a movie during or after textwork is motivating in itself. Moreover the juxtaposition of two different media opens up the possibility of using a variety of attention-grabbing methods and techniques. Henseler / Möller / Surkamp (2011: 239ff.) identify seven (more) benefits of integrating adaptations into TEFL:

- Media literacy, e. g. getting to know different processes of transformation
- Narrative competence, e. g. realizing that one and the same event may give rise to different stories

- Literary competence, e. g. recognising that the literary text is open to being interpreted in different ways for film
- Reading competence, e. g. reading part of the text source even more thoroughly
- Studying the staging dimension (drama adaptations), e. g. treating a play as merely a written text is avoided
- Aid in understanding, e. g. reading text passages as preparation for listening to difficult film material
- Authentic reason for speaking, e. g. expressing thwarted expectations

The case for adaptions in class seems clear, but there are a few problems which should not be ignored. Treating not only one, but two works takes up a lot of time. On top of that, the two authentic pieces often turn out to be rather complex in terms of their thematic content and linguistic level. Furthermore two likely consequences should be avoided:

Problems

2 Don'ts:
1. Reading should not be marginalized by viewing.
2. The tendency to judge the film as an inferior product is to be resisted.

12.2 Methodology

Apart from the general criteria for selection (ch. 1), a few adaptation-specific aspects cross one's mind. If you put reading on an equal footing, Kreutzer's type of *transformation* seems appropriate. The latter also lends itself to analyzing selected media changes. If more than one film version of a certain literary piece is available, cross-film differences can be highlighted, and the character of the source as a polysemous text void of a single meaning is made clear. Curricular requirements also have to be observed, often demanding the treatment of Shakespeare plays for advanced classes – and we may thank film directors for being so cooperative in producing a wealth of Bard adaptations.

Selection

As for the relationship between film and literature, there are at least four ways to explore that in the classroom: film on book,

Film – literature relationships

films (plural!) on book, book on film, author & film (cf. Thaler 2008).

Film on book

What first comes to one's mind is to use one book and its film adaptation. Much of classical and also modern literature is now easily available on DVD or other technical formats, so reading a book can be complemented by watching the audio-visual version and comparing the two media. Such a comparison is intended to identify the parallels and differences, to try to explain in an unbiased way why the director decided on the changes he made.

Films on book

A highly esteemed or popular book has often been adapted into several film versions by various directors, so a comparison of different movies can also be a rewarding approach. Individual directors pursue their own concepts about the aesthetics of a film, places and times may vary, actors interpret their roles differently, the release date influences production, a certain scene may be emphasized, deleted or inserted. A worthwhile attempt, in particular with various versions of a Shakespeare drama, is to choose one key scene and compare the different film adaptations. A grid with several criteria and empty columns for the different versions facilitates this elucidating yet demanding task.

Example: Kipling's *If*

Another example, which is not a drama and not by Shakespeare, would be the famous poem *If* (1895) by British Nobel laureate Rudyard Kipling. This moving evocation of self-control, stoicism, and the British "stiff upper lip" may sound a bit old-fashioned, but still enjoys widespread popularity amongst the British – and is often voted Britain's favourite poem. The poem's lines, "If you can meet with Triumph and Disaster / and treat those two impostors just the same" is written above the Centre Court players' entrance at the British tennis tournament Wimbledon. Thus presenting Roger Federer, the world's best tennis player, reciting his version of *If* may be a good idea (www.youtube.com/watch?v=jFcJPecO568). After a famous contemporary sportsman, the author himself is invited to read out his own – animated – poem (www.youtube.com/watch?v=wpcNFll5yOM). Finally, or even at the beginning, a version with the words of the poem inserted seems suitable (www.youtube.com/watch?v=pFaENAjk54s&feature=related).

Rudyard Kipling: *If*

If you can keep your head when all about you
Are losing theirs and blaming it on you;
If you can trust yourself when all men doubt you,
But make allowance for their doubting too:
If you can wait and not be tired by waiting,
Or being lied about, don't deal in lies,
Or being hated don't give way to hating,
And yet don't look too good, nor talk too wise;

If you can dream – and not make dreams your master;
If you can think – and not make thoughts your aim,
If you can meet with Triumph and Disaster
And treat those two impostors just the same:
If you can bear to hear the truth you've spoken
Twisted by knaves to make a trap for fools,
Or watch the things you gave your life to, broken,
And stoop and build 'em up with worn-out tools;

If you can make one heap of all your winnings
And risk it on one turn of pitch-and-toss,
And lose, and start again at your beginnings
And never breathe a word about your loss:
If you can force your heart and nerve and sinew
To serve your turn long after they are gone,
And so hold on when there is nothing in you
Except the Will which says to them: 'Hold on!'

If you can talk with crowds and keep your virtue,
Or walk with Kings – nor lose the common touch,
If neither foes nor loving friends can hurt you,
If all men count with you, but none too much:
If you can fill the unforgiving minute
With sixty seconds' worth of distance run,
Yours is the Earth and everything that's in it,
And – which is more – you'll be a man, my son!

www.kipling.org.uk/poems_if.htm

Book on film

Films are not only produced after a book (*Buchverfilmungen*), but in some cases books are written after a film (*Filmverbuchungen*). The screenplay of a movie can also be the source of derivative works like novels and plays. Such books on films quite often lack outstanding literary quality, yet they can help us to understand a difficult film. Moreover there are also differences between film and script to be discussed. The first books on films were Walt Disney's animated cartoons *Robin Hood* and *Cinderella* in the 1950, and later written versions of *E.T.*, *Raiders of the Lost Ark*, *The Land Before Time* and *Dead Poets Society* appeared. John Waters's films have been successfully staged as plays, and such a highly respected author like Graham Greene, with *The Third Man*, has worked from his own film ideas to a novel form.

Author & film

A fourth lit-film-relationship focuses on the creator of literary works, e. g. the *author docu*, which is a documentary about the life of a famous writer (cf. ch. 7). Such DVDs usually provide illuminating information on the political, social, and cultural background during the time in which an author lived, beyond a mere description of different stages in their life, thus contributing to a more complete understanding of their works. For example, Lingua Video has more than 25 bio docus from Austen to Wordsworth in stock. A related genre is called *biopic* (biography & motion picture), i.e. a movie depicting the life of a famous person, e. g. *Shakespeare in Love* (1998), *Capote* (2005), *Big Sur* (on Jack Kerouac, 2013), *The Story of Dr. Seuss* (2013), *Kill Your Darlings* (on Allen Ginsberg, 2013).

Combinations

Having two media at one's disposal, the question arises as to how to combine reading and viewing phases. The four approaches to watching a film (*straight through*, *segment*, *sandwich*, *clip*: ch. 8-11) can also be applied to the treatment of a book, i.e. you may read it in one go, split it into parts of fairly equal length, read some chapters and skip others, or select only one passage. A mathematical point of view would recognize 16 different combinations, and if you added the option of starting either the book or the film first, 32 different ways would be available to you. Following the traditional path, however, leads you to looking at the book first, and then viewing the whole film (straight through or segment approach & straight through approach). If you take "the one less traveled by" (Robert Frost), you may either read / view the exposition in detail and treat other passages more generally, or put a reading passage in between an older and a more modern version of a film, or start with a film trailer, or replace longer chapters of a book by faster film viewing, or ... – and that may have "made all the difference".

Analysis categories

When it comes to actually working with film adaptations, an analytical approach immediately springs to mind. When asking students to compare a film version with the text, we should basically tell them that there are the following categories:

- Identity, i.e. there are no changes
- Reduction, e. g. the whole story-line has been cut back
- Expansion, e. g. the film adds another character
- Omission, e. g. descriptive passages have been left out
- Replacement, e. g. a stream-of-consciousness passage has been replaced by voice-over commentary and close-ups
- Rearrangement, e. g. the film tells the story in flashback scenes
- Simplification, e. g. the complexity of a round character is reduced
- Shift of emphasis, e. g. a minor character gets more attention

A viewing grid, with separate columns for the different categories, makes related observation tasks simpler. Analytical work should, of course, not stop here, but ask why these changes have been made (form – function relation); however, it must also be made clear that there is no *form-to-function mapping*, i.e. a certain formal change does not always have the same consequence.

Analysis dimensions

Beside the *how*-question on the relations, the *what*-question on various analytical dimensions has to be specified for our learners. When comparing book and film / films, their attention may be drawn to these aspects:

- Story
- Characters
- Places
- Point of view
- Discourse

The parts of a film that are the most illuminating as far as contrastive analysis is concerned are the beginning and the end. In general, analytical work should not be content with isolating certain formal differences, but consider the unity of form, content and effect.

Activities

Comparing literature and film must not be reduced to analytical approaches only, though. Open, production-oriented and creative activities should also be represented in class. Lütge (2012: 77) and Surkamp (2004) emphasize the central significance of *imagining* the visual transformation of a printed text, for example finding ideas for the opening, selecting suitable scenes for adaptation, casting suitable actors, or designing a storyboard. Abraham (2009) favours writing activities, which may inspire both empathy and objectivity; he distinguishes between four types of writing: *clarifying writing* (e. g. writing summaries of film episodes in group work), *expressive writing* (e. g. keeping the diary of a film character), *poetic writing* (e. g. completing an ending which has been left open), and *rhetorical writing* (e. g. writing a film review). Further media such as bonus materials on the DVD, film posters, DVD covers, or film scripts may also be used.

12.3 Lessons

Sample 1

Title	William Shakespeare: *Hamlet*, III, 1 (soliloquy: *To be or not to be*)
Length	ca. 4 minutes
Synopsis	In this soliloquy, Hamlet ponders on the meaning of life. He asks himself if we should stay alive when life contains so many hardships, and concludes that the main reason why people do not commit suicide is the fear of death and uncertainty of what lies beyond life. Four film versions: 1. 1948, directed by and starring Sir Laurence Olivier 2. 1990, dir. by Franco Zeffirelli, st. Mel Gibson 3. 1996, dir. by / st. Kenneth Branagh 4. 2000, dir. by Michael Almereyda, st. Ethan Hawke
Topics	Life and death, action and procrastination, enduring and fighting, book and film, film and film, cinematic techniques
Level	Advanced
Time	135 minutes (3 lessons)

Procedure (Lütge 2012, Thaler 2008):

1. Written version of *To-be-or-not-to-be* soliloquy (III, 1)
a) Motivation: uniqueness of Hamlet
- Hazlitt: "Hamlet, that's us"
- one of Shakespeare's most quoted plays
- one of the world's literary icons
- the most frequently produced work in almost every western country
- Hamlet, the character: most discussed character in Western literature
- III, 1 soliloquy: the most popular passage
b) First reading (teacher)
c) Checking global comprehension
d) Providing a list of vocabulary annotations
e) Second reading (students)
f) Analysing the meaning
g) Personal evaluation

2. First film version of soliloquy (Sir Laurence Olivier, 1948)
a) Transition: role of Hamlet as the ultimate challenge for every ambitious actor
b) Blind listening (vision off)
c) Heartstorming (first impressions)
d) Sketching a rough film script
e) Second presentation (audio and vision on)
f) Discussing the visual representation (colour, camera, costumes, scenery ...)
g) Comparing with one's own suggestions (d)

3. Comparison of four film versions (Olivier, Gibson, Branagh, Hawke)
a) Handing out a grid (heading: visual effects, left column: 4 lines with the 4 films, middle column: colour / scenery / lighting / camera, right column: effect on viewer)
b) Viewing the 4 film clips (stopping after each version)
c) Filling in the grid
d) Discussing and evaluating the differences

4. Focused viewing: "Ay, there's the rub"
a) Repeated viewing of this passage (all four films)
b) Analysing the visual differences

5. Follow-up
Press conference with four students representing the four directors, other students as reporters

Sample 2

Title	*The Hunger Games* (novel: Suzanne Collins, 2008 / movie: Gary Ross, Suzanne Collins, Billy Ray, 2012)
Length	Book: 454 pages / movie: 142 minutes + extra material on DVD (completing the whole book and film is not necessary; a promising approach may be a double sandwich approach: excerpts from book and film.)
Synopsis	Every year in the ruins of what was once North America, the evil Capitol of the nation of Panem forces each of its twelve districts to send a teenage boy and girl to compete in the Hunger Games. As a punishment for some past uprising and a government intimidation tactic, the Hunger Games are a nationally broadcast event in which *Tributes* must fight with one another until one survivor remains. Katniss, the female protagonist, has to rely upon her sharp instincts as well as the mentorship of drunken former victor Haymitch Abernathy. If she is ever to return home to District 12, Katniss must make more than difficult decisions in the arena, which weigh survival against humanity, and life against love. (www.thehungergamesmovie.com/index.html?section=about)
Topics	Dystopias, media (entertainment, manipulation, reality TV), love, friendship, historical allusions (e. g. to ancient Rome), society, government vs freedom (obedience, conscience, rebellion)
Level	(Upper) intermediate / Advanced
Time	45 minutes (90' with part D) Teaching module: (at least) 9 lessons (of 45 minutes each)

Procedure:

Lesson 1

A. Pre-viewing
   (Preparatory homework: Read chapter 1)
   1. Is there anything that you would regard as 'unfilmable'? Why? (pair work)
   2. Collecting results (e. g. interior monologue, certain emotions etc.)

B. While-viewing
   1. First viewing of 'propaganda film' (90 seconds, included in main movie; available on YouTube; part of *extras* on DVD) ➤ collecting general impressions, explaining key vocabulary

2. Second viewing ➤ identifying the political agenda of certain games, the virtues that are advocated
3. Third viewing ➤ task: pay attention to the imagery and cinematic devices, make notes, and compare with your partner ➤ collecting and discussing results (see worksheet below)

C. Post-viewing
1. What kind of society is portrayed? (dystopia)
2. What genre of film is this? (propaganda film)
3. Why is this film included in the movie? (a rather long sequence from the book is put into a short *film within the film* to provide background information about Panem)

D. Follow-up (homework or second half of a double period)
Imagine you had to transfer the first chapter of the book into a film:
- Where would you start?
- What kind of shots do you need to capture the atmosphere, to convey the setting, to portray the characters?
- How much dialogue do you need?
- Would you add / leave out anything? Why?

Propaganda Film	
Text (script)	*Images / cinematic devices*
[Voice-over] War, terrible war. Widows, orphans, a motherless child. This was the uprising that rocked our land. Thirteen districts rebelled against the country that fed them, loved them, and protected them. Brother turned on brother until nothing remained.	• Skulls, rain → close-up, grey colours • Masked people in white protection suits, fire • Broken glass, destruction, lonely and dirty child → long shot, dark colours • Two sad looking, dirty children → close-up • Trash dump, running child, sad woman • Lonely person in rags • Broken doll in the mud in between broken dishes • Little boy and old, weak person • Series of very fast pictures: explosion, soldiers, building, destruction → overlapping images, grey-blue • Army, desert, explosion, ruins → pale-yellow • Nuclear explosion again → several overlapping images: black blossoming flower, mirroring the mushroom cloud → heroic music starts up

Then came the peace, hard fought, sorely won. The people rose up from the ashes and a new era was born. But freedom has a cost. When the traitors were defeated, we swore as a nation we would never know this treason again.	• Blue sky, golden cornfield → optimistic music, bird sounds, bright colours • Running child, clean, neatly dressed, happy → unusual camera angle • Father, lifting the child up → low angle • Laughing child → close-up • Older child looking straight into the camera • Happy couple, lying in the grass → floating camera movements • Young woman looking up → close-up
And so it was decreed that each year the various districts of Panem would offer up in tribute one young man and woman to fight to their death in a pageant of honor, courage and sacrifice. The lone victor, bathed in riches, would serve as a reminder of our generosity and our forgiveness. This is how we remember our past. This is how we safeguard our future.	• Red sealing wax dripping onto parchment • Handshake and sealing of document → overlapping images • Young man, hands and sword → close / detail • Various young, healthy and strong-looking people with weapons, dressed archaically, looking strong, healthy, proud, confident, standing on pedestals (staged like gladiators) → from close-up to full shot, camera movements: pan, tilt • Young man: victorious pose → camera circling him slowly • Cheering hands → overlapping images; sound: cheers, music: triumphant • Hands, pointing up, pastel-coloured sky, face of a black girl, sunset • National symbol of Panem

Ideas for further lessons

(First four lessons refer to part I of the novel)

Lesson 2: Opening

(based on chapter 1 of the novel and excerpts from the movie up to 00:18:00)

1. Discussing the results of the homework (1st lesson)
2. Watching the first 18 minutes of the film
3. Comparing students' suggestions (step 1 / homework) to the actual film:

- omissions
- characterization of protagonists
- narrator / point of view

- cinematic devices (hand camera, music, propaganda film ...)
- effect on the audience

Lesson 3: Looks in Panem

- Viewing minutes 18-33 (until the 'entrance of the tributes')
- Significance of the clothes in Panem
- Colours as a cinematic device
- Architecture of the Capitol
- (possibly) bonus-material / book excerpt: description of Caesar Flickerman

Lesson 4: Interviews with the tributes

- Preparatory homework: Read chapters 7 and 9
- Creating an interview: students are put into groups of three, the task is to devise one's own interview with the tributes, three roles: Caesar Flickerman and two tributes, interviews are prepared and acted out
- Watching the scene where the tributes are interviewed
- Comparing students' presentations with the film

Topics for **parts II and III** (chapter 10ff.):

- Bread and games – Panem and Rome and everytown
- "Star-crossed lovers" – true love and calculated stratagem
- Conformity and resistance – Panem and Germany and ...
- Appearances – seeming and being
- Games and competitions – win or lose
- Society and class – the *haves* vs the *have nots*
- Individuality – strengths and skills
- Sacrifice – you or me

Tasks

1. Mention five forms of film adaptations and give one example of each.
2. Choose one of your examples, preferably a short one, and sketch a teaching sequence based on it.
3. Do you like the first lesson on *The Hunger Games*? Say why (not).

13 Children's Films

Do you think the use of films is appropriate for young learners? State your opinion.

13.1 Theory

Definition

Children's films are those productions that are aimed at children aged up to 12 years (Völcker 2005), though they may be appreciated by all age groups, and are usually rated 'G' ("suitable for general audience").

Characteristics

They focus on child-related themes, offer "mainly or entirely a child's point of view" (Bazalgette / Staples 1995: 96), are non-offensive and entertaining, and usually teach a lesson or moral, for example, good triumphs over evil. Plots often involve a journey, characters include helpful and friendly creatures as well as supernatural beings, the setting can be a fantastic, far-away world. The cast usually comprises child actors / actresses and non-human characters, i.e. animals with dogs or puppies being the most prominent choice.

Genres

As for genres, a first distinction refers to animated and non-animated (live action) children's films – although according to Phillips (2009: 224), animation is a technique for making a film rather than a type of film. Animation is usually created by photographing a series of objects, with the rapid display of a sequence of images (standard succession at 24 frames per second) creating an illusion of movement (Borwell / Thompson 2003: 162). Filmmakers may 'animate', i.e. bring to life, flat, two-dimensional objects (drawings, paintings, illustrations, photographs), and three-dimensional objects (e. g. puppets), or use computer imaging.

According to Wojik-Andrews (2000: 161) the major children's film genres are "realism, fantasy and animation, as well as musicals, war, sports and literary adaptations". Lukasz-Aden / Strobel (1988) suggest the following categories:

Genres of Children's Films	
Category	*Examples*
Adventure films	*Treasure Island* (1950) *The Goonies* (1985)
Animals and nature	*The Golden Seal* (1983) *Sacred Planet* (2005)
Animation films	*Wallace & Gromit* (1989) *Madagascar* (2005)
Children's detectives	*Sammy's Super-T-Shirt* (1977) *The Battle of Billies Pond* (1978)
Fairy tales	*The Thief of Bagdad* (1940) *Tom Thumb* (1958)
Fantasy vs reality	*Mary Poppins* (1964) *Secret Garden* (1990)
History	*Hope and Glory* (1987) *Oliver Twist* (1948)
Indians	*Broken Arrow* (1950) *White Feather* (1955)
Literary adaptations	*Alice in Wonderland* (2010) *The Wonderful Wizard of Oz* (2011)
Musicals	*Mary Poppins* (1964) *Bugsy Malone* (1975)
Science fiction	*E.T.* (1982) *Aliens in the Attic* (2009)
Slapstick	*The Kid* (1921) *The Golden Rush* (1924/25)

With regard to production style, you may also distinguish between mainstream and art house films (Völcker 2005: 31), the latter being "experimental films" or "ambitious films", which are not produced for entertainment purpose only, but often screened at festivals and less frequently in cinemas.

Themes

The topics in children's films are more varied than one might think. They include:

- Love & friendship ➤ *WALL-E* (2008)
- Family ➤ *Home Alone* (1990)
- Superhero ➤ *Superman* (1978)
- Growing up & school ➤ *To Sir with Love* (1967)
- Future & space ➤ *Star Wars: The Clone Wars* (2008)

- Life values ➤ *It's a Wonderful Life* (1946)
- War & peace ➤ *The Diary of Anne Frank* (1959)
- Self-awareness ➤ *Kung Fu Panda* (2008)
- Journey ➤ *The Wonderful Wizard of Oz* (1939)
- Sports ➤ *Angel in the Outfield* (1994)
- Hopes & dreams ➤ *Madagascar* (2005)
- Christmas ➤ *The Muppet Christmas Carol* (1992)
- Environment ➤ *Ice Age* (2002)
- Animals ➤ *Black Stallion* (1979)
- Miracle ➤ *Miracle on 34th Street* (1947)
- Racial inequality ➤ *To Kill a Mockingbird* (1962)
- Social arrangements ➤ *Aladin* (1992)

History

The history of children's films first started in the silent era of cinema. According to Goldstein / Zornows (cited in Wojik-Andrews 2000: 54), they originated in 1898, when Louis Lumière's *Le Déjeuner de Bébé* was screened. In the early 1920's Walt Disney introduced the first cartoon characters like Donald Duck, Goofy and Mickey Mouse. The "Golden Age of Hollywood" (1927-1941) saw three significant literary adaptations: *Snow White and Seven Dwarfs* (1937), *Gulliver's Travels* (1939), and *Pinocchio* (1940). Many children's films that have become classics of the genre were released during the late 1940s and early 1950s. In the 1990s the studios proceeded to produce adaptations of classic works, e. g. *Beauty and the Beast* (1991), *Aladin* (1992), *The Secret Garden* (1993). Another striking development in the 1990s was that of computer generated imaging and animation (*Toy Story*, 1990), which was refined in the 2000s: *Shrek* (2001), *Ice Age* (2002), *Madagascar* (2005), *Cars* (2005), *Kung Fu Panda* (2008), *Brave* (2012).

Benefits

Films may already be used in young learners' classrooms. Children relish language learning with audiovisual material, as it creates an enjoyable learning environment. Video can communicate meaning better than other media, as visual clues aid comprehension, learners see who / what is speaking, where the conversation is taking place, and what the speakers are doing. Studying body language and other non-verbal communication is beneficial particularly for very young learners, who are still experiencing the world around them. Young children also like to hear stories again and again, learn by absorbing and imitating, gain confidence through repetition, while watching films several times (ibid.). Children's films, moreover, are not too complicated and have a reduced number of actors and settings.

Problems

Objections to confronting young learners with foreign language films may be raised, though. Is it really necessary to start FBLL in the primary classroom? Can they understand authentic English in the first place? Are the themes and contents appropriate for our pupils? "Videos dürfen auf keinen Fall Inhalte vermitteln, die allenfalls für Vorschulkinder interessant sind" (Waas / Hamm 2004: 56).

The crux – not just for primary pupils – often lies in the content – language gap: Simple language videos may be perceived as too 'childish' with regard to contents, thematically appropriate films contain too much advanced language input.

13.2 Methodology

Sources

The lists above already mention several children's films, some of which, however, are beyond the linguistic (and cognitive) level of primary school children. If you are looking for audiovisual material suitable for beginners, the following resources may be helpful:

- DVDs for sale, e. g. *Spider, Spot, Pingu, Mr Ben, Eric Carle stories, Wallace and Gromit, Curious George, The Race*

Abb. 13 | Wallace & Gromit

- TV programmes: digital English language channels (e. g. TV series like *Horrid Henry: Sports Day, Grandpa in My Pocket: The Wonderful World of Mr Whoops*), EL programmes of federal states' channels, e. g. *Playtime* for 5+ learners (www.br.de/fernsehen/br-alpha/sendungen/playtime/playtime102.html)
- Film publishers' brochures, e. g. Lingua Video (http://lingua-video.com/index.php?l=39)
- Coursebook publishers, e. g. *Playway* (video, DVD)
- Websites, e. g. YouTube provides lots of useful short clips for younger learners (for example, numerous versions of the *Alphabet Song*) including adaptations of children's books (*The Very Hungry Caterpillar, Where the Wild Things Are*). Dvolver Moviemaker (www.dfilm.com/moviemaker/make.html) encourages young children to make their own animated movie – comedy, drama, or love story – and send it to their friends. In Germany, *Hamburger Bildungsserver* (www.bildungsserver.hamburg.de), *Landesmedienzentrum Baden-Württemberg* (www.lmz-bw.de), *Medienzentrum Bielefeld* (www.medienzentrum-bielefeld.de), and *Planet Schule* (www.planet-schule.de) have compiled weblinks as well as lists of films on DVD suitable especially for primary school children.

Selection

Materials for young pupils must, above all, be appropriate to the learners' age (cf. ch. 1.10). The film should have substantial visual support ("... when using authentic video make sure they have a high visual content ...": Phillips 1995: 133), should be set in a familiar environment, have good sound, and are accompanied by further teaching materials (basis for activities, recycling language patterns and words of the film, a transcript, pull-out sheets, sheets of coloured paper etc.). It helps if the language input is not too dense, words and structures are simple, background sounds are missing, and a limited number of speakers speak with a clear pronunciation (RP) as well as at slow speed.

Methodological principles

Young learners, in particular, need variety. Considering the attention span of primary school children, it is also advisable to keep an English lesson sequence below 30-35 minutes. The following star advocates 10 further methodological principles for young learners (Thaler 2012):

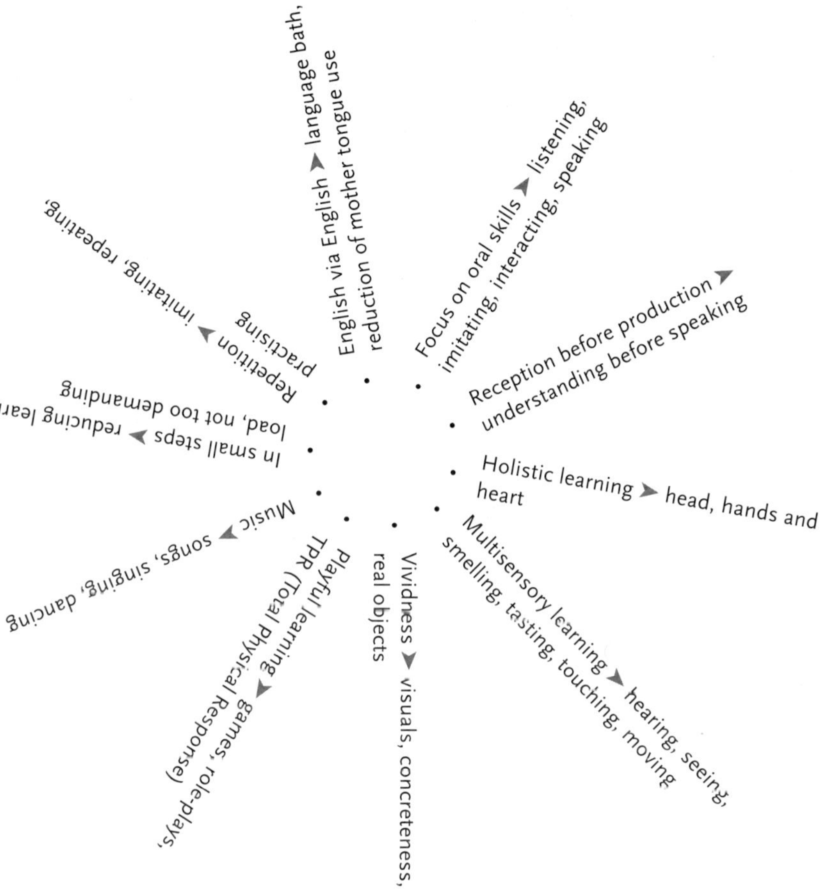

Activities

Before watching a film in class, children must be prepared for this challenging task. Questions to elicit the pupils' background knowledge should be asked, the context for the dialogue in the video explained and key vocabulary introduced. The activities should be based on oral skills as there is hardly any emphasis on reading and writing. Simple while-viewing activities should focus on the content of the film. The five *w-questions* can help children understand what is going on in the film: *Who? When? Where? What? Why?* Post-viewing activities lead to deeper comprehension and an improvement in vocabulary, grammar, pronunciation, and much more. "These tasks should help children understand the video in more detail, and should focus on both the language and the pictures" (Phillips 1995: 135). Practising and playing with the foreign language remains the major aim, and this can be done with spot-the-lie summaries, true-false statements, role plays, acting out roles and many other techniques.

4 P's A structural pattern similar to the *5 W's* is called the *4 P's*. Children are said to be especially interested in people, plot, places and the point (or problems).

The 4 P's	
Persons	• Who is the main character? • Can you describe him / her? • How old is he / she? What does he / she look like? What is he / she wearing? • Is he happy / sad / nervous ...? • What do they say? Can you repeat what X says? • Do you like them?
Places	• Where are the people? • Do the places change? • What time of day is it in this place?
Plot	• What happens? • How does it start / end? • Do you like the ending? • Who is telling the story?
Point (Problem)	• What is the message? What is the lesson you can learn? • Is there any problem? • Is it a happy end? Why? Who wins? • What is the moral? Do you agree?

13.3 Lessons

Sample 1

Title	*The Very Hungry Caterpillar by Eric Carle* (www.youtube.com/watch?v=nKKdwGwOlK8)
Length	6 minutes
Synopsis	The film depicts a green baby caterpillar being hatched from an egg. Trying to get as much food as possible, it consumes enormous amounts of various types of food until it feels sated. Then it spins a cocoon in which it remains for the following two weeks. Later, the caterpillar appears as an extremely beautiful butterfly with large, colourful wings.
Topics	Food, days of the week, repetition of numbers (1-10), development of animals
Level	Beginners
Time	35 minutes

Procedure:

A. Pre-viewing
1. Repetition: numbers 1-10 (choral speaking)
2. Transition: Who knows the book *The Very Hungry Caterpillar*?
3. Vocabulary: food

B. While-viewing
1. TPR task: Stand up when you hear food words (Total Physical Response)
2. First viewing (and TPR)
3. Second viewing
4. Summary (whole class)

C. Post-viewing
1. Gapped weekdays (worksheet: days of the week, first letter deleted)
2. Pronunciation (days of the week)
3. Food and days (worksheet: learners match the days of the week to what the hungry caterpillar eats; they cut out the fruits and stick them to the days).

D. Homework
Picture colouring: Children colour a worksheet which displays the different items from the story. They cut them out and glue them on a drawing done in a previous art lesson. The productions are presented in the next lesson.

Sample 2

Title	*Alphabet Song* (www.youtube.com/watch?v=Er_dDJDAPUo)
Length	4:21 minutes
Synopsis	In this classic clip from *Sesame Street*, Don Music writes the *Alphabet Song*, gets stuck regularly, but receives – accidental – help from Kermit and others. The music for this funny *Alphabet Song* is also the tune for *Twinkle Twinkle Little Star*.
Topics	ABC, learning the alphabet with music, repetition and a famous animated children's series
Level	Beginners
Time	20 minutes

Procedure:

1. Teacher starts to sing the ABC song until the letter F, then pretends to not know the next letter, gets furious and cries: "I'll never learn the ABC, never, never!"
2. Transition: T needs help from Kermit & Co. from Sesame Street.
3. Clip is played straight through.
4. T and whole class try to do the alphabet.
5. Clip is played a second time, and stopped every time the musician gets stuck. ➤ letters are repeated, help from Kermit & Co. is explained, next letter is guessed at.
6. Class chain: Every pupil says one letter.

Tasks

1. Mention six methodological principles for using films with young learners.
2. Choose a short children's film, or an excerpt from a full-length children's movie, and sketch a lesson design for primary classrooms.
3. Discuss whether to use films with young children in their first two years of English.

Conclusion

14 Assessment

Should we assess FBLL? If so, how?

14.1 Theory

Backwash effect

Testing is anything but popular with our students. So do we really have to assess film literacy? Establishing a *test-free film zone* sounds tempting, but unfortunately the so-called *backwash effect* claims that what is being tested is taught and learned – and, vice versa, what is not being tested, is not learned (and taught). So if we refrain from setting film tests, the value placed on FBLL will diminish.

Necessity of assessment

Apart from the backwash effect, further arguments speak for assessing film literacy: achievement (How far have learners progressed in relation to the objectives in the curriculum?), feedback for teachers (What have my students not understood yet?), feedback for learners (In what areas must I try harder?), and – of course – the requirements of the official guidelines and curricula. The Common European Framework of Reference for Languages (Council of Europe 2001) mentions "Watching TV programmes and films" (cf. ch. 1), and national or federal state curricula have explicitly listed media literacy and, in particular, listening-viewing.

Quality features

If we have to test, we should do it well. Good assessment practice adheres to the three traditional characteristics, i.e. validity, reliability, objectivity, and a number of other features such as feasibility (practicality of assessment tools in view of teachers' workload), variety (combination of discrete-point testing, integrative testing and pragmatic testing), and mode duality (written and oral forms of assessment). A test is valid if it really tests what it claims to test, so if our goal is film literacy, and an exam intends to assess the full range of it, true / false statements on cinematic devices would not be sufficient. Of the three areas of audiovisual competence (knowledge, skills, attitudes), the one covering personal attitudes is certainly hardest to evaluate. To achieve a high degree of reliability and objectivity, teachers need a precise and practical set of criteria which guides them in assessing students' output, with the most basic set consisting of two criteria, i.e. content and language.

Educational standards

Unfortunately there is a lack of empirical research on how to assess film literacy due to the novelty of this concept, and the descriptions in educational documents are of restricted scope and value. As to listening-viewing, the CEF confines itself to giving a simple, generalised scale on "Watching TV programmes and films", and the educational standards of Germany for the first foreign language (KMK 2004), for example, put can-do statements for listening and listening-viewing together, implying that it is one and the same competence. The desiderata for research and educational policy are evident (Porsch / Grotjahn / Tesch 2010): describing the constructs (What is film literacy? What is listening-viewing competence?) ➤ drafting can-do statements on the various levels ➤ specifiying appropriate tests (task formats, target groups etc.) ➤ developing suitable tasks ➤ piloting and revising tasks ➤ measuring target competence(s), level-based feedback ➤ evaluating the results didactically ➤ planning teaching.

14.2 Methodology

Test formats

For want of cogent empirical research data and convincing educational policy guidelines, teachers need to take recourse to general information about test formats. The CEF (Council of Europe 2001: chapter 9) mentions various types of assessment, several of which are also relevant for film literacy:

- *continuous assessment* (students' performances throughout the course) and *fixed-point assessment* (based on an exam taking place on a particular day)
- *holistic assessment* (making a global synthetic judgement) and *analytical assessment* (looking at different aspects separately, breaking down evaluation into a set of criteria)
- *criterion-referenced assessment* (with regard to the degree of achieving certain learning targets) and *norm-referenced assessment* (students assessed in relation to their peers in class, bell curve)
- *teacher assessment* (teacher as *grade-giver*) and *peer* as well as *self-assessment*

As film literacy covers a lot of different components, including cinematic knowledge, special skills and appropriate attitudes, the choice of test formats needs to reflect this wide range.

Assessment categories

A lot of national guidelines demand the three levels of comprehension and reproduction, analysis and reorganization, as well as evaluation and creation. The nature of audiovisual literacy suggests a refinement and expansion to comprise the following five categories.

Assessing Film Literacy

Category	*Examples*
Listening-viewing comprehension	• Multiple choice items • True-false statements • Matching exercises • Gapped texts • Odd one out • Error spotting etc.
Film analysis	• Viewing grids • Questions on form and function of cinematic techniques • Applying film terminology etc.
Evaluation	• Comments • Film reviews • Essays etc.
Creation	• Making a film magazine • Producing a film • Visual, auditory, audio-visual, scenic forms
Process orientation	• Portfolios • Film diaries • Self-evaluation sheets etc.

Suggestions

To conclude, a few suggestions may help teachers prepare, design and administer tests on film literacy:

- The notion of the film literacy construct determines test specifications and expected competences.
- Test formats and expected competences must be made clear to the learners well in advance of the actual test (transparency!).

- The basis of the tests consists of authentic audiovisual materials.
- Various types of films (feature films, TV programmes, weather forecasts, TV news, commercials, trailers, sketches etc.) should be used in the long run.
- The length of the film is dependent on the learners' level, but short films or excerpts from longer films (under 6 minutes) are to be preferred (risk of cognitive overload!).
- The requirements follow a qualitative and quantitative progression (Henseler / Möller / Surkamp 2011: 24ff.).
- Over a longer period, a variety of item formats should be applied.
- Reading and writing need to be restricted when testing listening-viewing competences (validity!).
- The purpose of viewing must be spelt out to the learners before viewing begins (global or detailed comprehension?).
- The film (excerpt) may be presented once or twice.
- One, two or even three short films may be employed with separate tasks.
- Learners must be given some time to read through the instructions and tasks before the film is started.
- Apart from the rather conventional test formats, more student-centred ways of evaluation have been recommended in recent years, like portfolios or film diaries.

14.3 Samples

Test 1

Title	*London Now* (DVD) (http://bildungsstandards.bildung-rp.de/uploads/media/Beispielaufgaben_Kl_8_Englisch_01.pdf)
Length	20' (the whole DVD)
Synopsis	The film gives an overview of modern London and is spoken in clear American English. The individual chapters can be used as separate clips, e. g. City of London. The DVD also contains statements on "Do you like London", an interview with a bank manager and a quiz.
Topics	London, listening-viewing competence

Level	Intermediate (Germany: grade 8)
Time	Part I: 15 minutes (incl. viewing: 4') Part II: 15 minutes (incl. viewing: 4')

Procedure:
The sample tests by the educational authorities of Rhineland Palatiate suggest two parts.

Part I: Multiple choice
Students watch the film on London and tick off the right answers. There are twelve questions with three answers each.

Part II: Ticking likes and dislikes
Do you like London? Find out what people like and dislike about London. Tick those likes and dislikes that you heard in the film.

People like London because ...	*People don't like London because ...*
London is an exciting town	people are not friendly
there are people from all over the world	it is expensive
there is much to do	it is too fast
it is fast moving	there are only black people
it is a great city	it is dirty
it is quiet	there are so many tourists
it is old-fashioned	the people are not so friendly
there are a lot of skyscrapers	it is too big
of the excellent shopping facilities	there are only business people
of its history	there is too much traffic
of its museums and galleries	it is boring

Test 2

Title	*Dead Poets Society*: Keating's poem recital lesson (introduced by a short scene with Todd working in his room, DVD, minutes 51-55)
Length	4 ½ minutes
Synopsis	Todd tries to write a poem, does not succeed, however, and so tears the paper in frustration. In the English class the next day the students have to present their assignments, i.e. read out the poems they have written. Knox recites a love poem addressed to Chris; he looks disappointed because he feels he has not found the appropriate words to express his love; Mr Keating, however praises this effort because Knox has dealt with a major theme both in poetry and in life: love.

	Mr Hopkins reads out a very short and simple poem; Keating rejects this poem, not because it deals with a simple theme, but because it is ordinary. Inspired by Mr Keating, Todd finally overcomes his inhibitions and dares to speak about his fears and nightmares in public.
Topics	Education, school, poetry, film literacy
Level	Upper intermediate (if this sequence has been dealt with only generally in class before, students' pre-knowledge is not too deep.)
Time	90 minutes

Procedure:
First the test sheet is handed out, time is set aside for students to read the questions, then the film segment is shown, finally the questions have to be answered.

Tasks:
1. Give a short summary of the contents of this film segment. Also consider how the beginning and the end of the sequence are linked.
2. Analyse the cinematic means which are employed to show what Todd learns in the lesson.
3. Comment on the teaching methods and techniques used by Mr Keating in this lesson.
4. Write a short diary entry about your reactions to this English lesson. You can choose Todd's, Mr Hopkins' or Knox' point of view.

Test 3

Title	*Monty Python's Life of Brian*: Finale (stopping the film before song sets in)
Length	6 minutes
Synopsis	The final scene shows Brian suffering on the cross, and the reactions of various groups (PFJ, Judean People's Front, Judith, Mandy) to his affliction.
Topics	Religious and political satire, film literacy
Level	Advanced (test applied after the whole film has been dealt with in class)
Time	90 minutes

Procedure:
First the test sheet is handed out, time is set aside for students to read the questions, then the film segment is shown, finally the questions have to be answered.

Tasks:

1. *Context*
   Put this scene into its context, i.e. describe briefly what happened immediately before and what will happen after it.
2. *Listening-viewing comprehension*
   2.1 What do Gregory (the man on the cross with his wife) and the saintly passer-by complain about?
   2.2 How do the following groups and people react to Brian being crucified: PFJ (Reg et al.), Judean People's Front, Judith, Mandy? In what way is their reaction similar?
3. *Analysis*
   In what way is the PFJ's reaction in accordance with their behaviour throughout the story? What might Monty Python be criticizing in general here?
4. *Humour*
   Choose three forms of humour in this excerpt and explain their function.
5. *Composition*
   Choose one of the three topics and write a composition of about 100 words.
   a) Was it justified to accuse the film of blasphemy?
   b) What parallels between the film and Christ's life according to the Gospel can you detect?
   c) Should a film like *The Life of Brian* be taught at school?

Tasks

1. Mention four categories of how to test film literacy and give one example each.
2. Do either test 2 or 3.
3. Design a test on FBLL in a class of your choice.

15 Balanced FBLL

Try and draw a conclusion: How are you going to teach English with films in the future?

The aim of Balanced Teaching is to avoid the one-sidedness of both instructivism and constructivism in order to enable balance, change of methods, variety and effectiveness.

Balanced Teaching

In a narrow sense, *Balanced Teaching* refers to a synthesis of closed and open learning arrangements (methods), in a broader sense, a productive equilibrium should also be aimed for in fields like objectives, competences, lesson structure, classroom discourse, teacher roles, learner roles, activities, interaction patterns, mood, tempo, and assessment. Such a *Balanced Teaching* is what an overwhelming majority of teachers want (Thaler 2008: 292ff.).

Balance in FBLL

The art of Film-Based Language Learning also seems to lie in striking a fair balance between teacher-fronted instructivism and student-centred constructivism, between guidance and autonomy (also see Lütge 2012: 11). In the context of audio-visual media, a balance must also be found concerning:

- Purpose: You should not analyse a certain film scene to death – learners may get very bored. Some scenes need repeated viewings with detailed observation tasks, whilst in other lesson stages viewing for gist is more suitable.
- Media: The standard procedure is to work on one film. But if you have more film versions available, inter-textuality or intermediality can be encouraged. And why not make use of further media and materials such as film posters, DVD covers, filmscripts, songs etc..
- Activities: Closed exercises should be supplemented by open tasks, cognitive and analytical approaches by productive and creative ones (film analysis & film experience). As far as mental activities are concerned, different cognitive skills are to be promoted, such as remembering (➤ e. g. filling in a table with the 4 P's), describing (➤ e. g. freeze frame: What does he look like?), summarizing (➤ e. g. retelling the story in a class

chain), guessing (➤ e. g. silent viewing: What might the characters be saying?) predicting (➤ e. g. upside down comprehension: questions on the content are answered before viewing), explaining (➤ e. g last scene: What has caused this situation?), analyzing (➤ e. g. form and function of cinematic techniques), cooperating (➤ e. g. split viewing), and transforming (➤ e. g. changing film into short story).

- Place: The desk-bound approach should be complemented by extramural English. It is listening-viewing in particular which demands independent study outside the classroom. Keeping a film diary (similar to a reading diary), in which learners make notes of plot, characters and film techniques, helps them to structure their impressions and document their autonomous work.
- Goal: The ultimate goal with films in TEFL lies in a balance between learning and enjoying (*Lernen & Lust*), work and pleasure, improving and savouring film literacy. Presenting a film for entertainment only, without any clear instructions, contributes as little to film literacy as analyzing every single scene in the same monotonous manner. If learners' awareness for cinematic devices has been raised, they will recognize formal techniques even in a state of passive viewing. Even so, films in English language teaching should also be allowed to entertain and motivate boys and girls as they do so in their leisure time.

Balanced Film-Based Language Learning

Closed Teaching		*Open Learning*
teacher-fronted		student-centred
intensive viewing		viewing for gist
one film		inter-mediality
closed exercises		open tasks
deskbound approach		extramural study
film analysis		film experience
film orientation		learner orientation
object (thing)		subject (person)
learning		enjoying

motivating & effective
FBLL

If this balance is taken care of, motivating and effective film-based language teaching can be achieved.

You cannot cater for all dimensions of balance in every teaching sequence, but over a longer period an attempt at a fair balance should be made. To finish with, a double lesson on R.E.M.'s classic music video *Everybody Hurts* illustrates one way of striking a balance: The first lesson is rather closed (teacher-guided, triple viewing), whereas the second lesson is quite open (student-centred, using the carousel approach: learning at stations).

Title	R.E.M.: *Everybody Hurts*
Length	5 minutes
Synopsis	In this classic music video, the band is stuck in a traffic jam at one of those highway interchanges where roads and bridges cross each other on several levels, reminding one of Fritz Lang's silent movies. The camera zooms in on the other cars' occupants with their wistful faces – and subtitles of their thoughts appear on screen. At the end, singer Michael Stipe gets out of his car and wanders between the lanes, posing like Messiah and begging: "Everybody hurts – so hold on." The other people also leave their cars, walking instead and finally vanishing. A puzzled voice-over announces that she has never seen anything like that.
Topics	Big city life, traffic, cars, helplessness, behaviour in moments of crisis, enduring vs changing
Level	Upper intermediate
Time	90 minutes

Procedure:

I. First lesson
(teacher guided analysis)

1. Lead-in: Speculating on the title of the song

2. After the 1st viewing: general comprehension
   a) Summarize the story-line of this music video.
   b) What does the newscaster at the end of the video say?

3. During the 2nd viewing: reading people's minds

Whenever the verbal representations of people's thoughts are freeze-framed, read the lines, characterize the people and speculate about the background of their thoughts.

The 16 ideas read as follows:

They're all stuck - Look at me - Silence is gray - Silence is golden - Silence is a stone in my mouth - Nobody can see me - I had no idea - They're going to miss me - Here we go again - What is she thinking? - 17 years - If I had a gun - How'm I gonna do this? - Lead me to the rock that is higher than I - They that sow in tears shall reap in joy - Stop singing! Stop singing! Stop singing! - You die, you turn to dust - I'll talk when I want to - Why won't you answer me? - Vamos a perder toda nuestra dignidad - No tenemos mas tempo - No more tears - Then can I grieve at grievances foregone - She's gone. Goodbye - There's nothing I can do - Leave me alone

4. During the 3rd viewing: identifying key phrases
While you are watching the video, focus on the lyrics in the subtitles (bottom of monitor) and take notes of the phrases that seem most important for the message of the song.

5. Discussing results

II. Second lesson
(*station learning*)

Learning Point 1: Do you remember the lyrics?
Try to remember the 10 missing words in the following lyrics. If you can't, discuss the most sensible guesses within your group.

R.E.M.: *Everybody Hurts*

When the day is long and the night, the night is yours alone,

when you're sure you've had enough of this life, well .... on.

Don't let yourself go, everybody cries and everybody .... sometimes.

Sometimes everything is wrong. Now it's time to .... along.

When your day is night alone, (hold on, hold on)

if you feel like .... go, (hold on)

when you think you've had too much of this life, well hang on.

Everybody hurts. Take .... in your friends.

Everybody hurts. Don't throw your hand. Oh, no. Don't throw your hand.

If you feel like you're ...., no, no, no, you are not alone

If you're on your .... in this life, the days and nights are long,

when you think you've had too much of this .... to hang on.

Well, everybody hurts sometimes,

everybody .... And everybody hurts sometimes.

And everybody hurts sometimes. So, hold on, hold on.

Hold on, hold on. Hold on, hold on. Hold on, hold on. (repeat & fade)

(Everybody hurts. You are not ....)

Learning Point 2: What is the message of this music video?
Discuss what the overall meaning of this music video is. Each of you must take one of the following six chairs. After a short statement by the five experts, discuss what they have claimed.
Expert 1: *lyrics* (verses, chorus, intention)
Expert 2: *ideas* (drivers' and occupants' minds)
Expert 3: *visuals* (situation, plot, ending, cinematography)
Expert 4: *music* (sound, melody, instruments, voice)
Expert 5: *context* (parallels to other texts, songs, films)
Chair 6: *chairperson*

Learning Point 3: Is suicide the answer?
Talk in pairs. One is a person who ponders suicide, the other is a psychiatrist trying to help him. After two minutes each patient gets up, moves to the next chair and talks to another psychiatrist.

Learning Point 4: What about another R.E.M. video?
Which of the following four R.E.M. videos would you like to see:
- DRIVE
- MAN ON THE MOON
- THE SIDEWINDER SLEEPS TONITE
- CRUSH WITH EYELINER

Your task at this station is twofold:
- While watching the second R.E.M. video, try out the technical features of DVD on your own (direct access to your track, subtitles, fast forward/rewind, digital zoom, bookmarking). Your teacher will assist you.
- Draw a comparison with EVERYBODY HURTS (parallels, differences).

Tasks

1. Mention four areas of Balanced FBLL.
2. Design a lesson which adheres to the principles of Balanced FBLL.
3. Write an email to the author (thaler@phil.uni-augsburg.de), evaluating the benefits and deficiencies of this volume. Your feedback is welcome. Thank you very much!

Suggested answers for the tasks

Chapter 1

1.

time conflict, language conflict, reception conflict, goal conflict, technology conflict
e. g. language conflict ➤ ways to alleviate the problem: saying no to "having-to-understand-everything-attitude", film selection adapted to learners' level, simple plots, slow and clear pronunciation (RP), repeated viewings, pre-viewing activities, few discrepancies between words and visuals ...

2.

yes: partly good to understand, humorous dialogues, intercultural learning, two people from different cultures, language awareness, similarities between German and English, cinematic quality (Jarmusch) ...
no: no standard pronunciation, deficient language (Müller-Stahl), slang and taboo words ...

3.

individual answers

Chapter 2

1.

cinematic devices: (a) shot (b) medium (c) extreme close-up (d) static shot (e) Panning (f) tilting (g) tracking shot (h) crane shot (i) Zooming (j) point-of-view shot (k) establishing shot (l) over-the-shoulder shot (m) eye-level shot (n) bird's eye view (o) worm's eye view

2.

possible learning objectives:
- knowledge: Anglo-French relationships (historical background)
- skills: Listening-viewing comprehension, mediation (French signs – English, German – English), creating (acting out in three roles)
- attitudes: enjoyment of humorous films, intercultural awareness

3.

yes: climax of teaching film literacy, P decalogue of media literacy, creative change from daily routine ...

no: time pressure, poor quality of final product, discipline / management problems ...

Chapter 3

1.

The seven approaches are called lyrics-first-approach, sound-first-approach, vision-first-approach, vision-off-approach, sound-off-approach, lyrics-off-approach and all-codes-approach. For their use, see p. 65).

2.

While-viewing task 1, solutions to gapped text: a) movie scenes, b) sirens, c) Broadway, d) made of, e) brandnew, f) will inspire, g) On the avenue, h) melting pot, i) Brooklyn Bridge, j) by any means, k) look pretty, l) compare, m) lighters
While-viewing task 2, selection of places / things shown in the video: Empire State Building, Hudson River, Manhattan skyline, lots of lights, cabs, cars driving down the roads and lots of people in the streets ➤ reference to noise; ships, Central Station, Brooklyn Bridge, marquees, Broadway, fireworks, Times Square, Central Park, subway, graffiti, rundown areas, New York by day and night ➤ reference to curfew, New York in different seasons, Alicia Keys at the piano, people looking at the Empire State Building ➤ reference to dreams / Empire State of Mind
Post-viewing question 3: The city is presented as a place that is amazing, beautiful, bright, crowded, fresh, incredible, interesting, magnificent, modern, noisy, perfect, pleasant, remarkable, shiny, sensational, terrific, unique, unusual, vibrant ...
The kind of music is easy listening, R&B, anthem, ballad.
The timbre (sound) of the song is bright, dark, full, gentle, light, loud, melodious, resonant, rhythmic, romantic, rounded, soft, strident, strong, thin, warm ...
The music and the pictures are exciting, relaxing, stimulating, enlightening, exhilarating, frightening, invigorating ...
They stir your imagination, make you happy, lift your mood and spirits, make you more alert ...

Alicia Keys sings a love song to her city. After listening to the song and seeing the video, I share / don't share her fascination.
I have a crush on the city now / can imagine living there / want to go and see the city.
I understand that she is in love with her native city, but I don't want to go there because I don't like such big cities / the noise / so many people ...
Task 4: This is a reference to Frank Sinatra and his famous song about New York (suggestion: Give the students the full lyrics of the song or tell them to listen to the song at home). ➤ Singer says that if you are successful in New York, you can be successful in any other city.
I agree because NY is such a big city that it is difficult to get on there, there are many artists, so there is a lot of competition ...
I don't agree because Los Angeles and its cultural industry is way more important, so you have to be successful there, there are many cities worldwide that are bigger and where life is tougher, so you have to make it there ...
Task 5: Term itself is a neologism and was invented by the songwriter ➤ a newly coined word blending the terms Empire State Building and state of mind (blend word), refers to the height of the Empire State Building and describes a positive state of mind (the city of New York makes you feel good and lifts your spirits up as high as the Empire State Building), in an Empire State of Mind you have high ambitions / reach for the stars / try to pursue your dreams, on top of the Empire State Building you have a good view over the "concrete jungle where dreams are made of", which helps you to pursue your dreams.

3.

e. g. racism in USA: You could use "American Skin (41 Shots)" by Bruce Springsteen. It deals with the issue that more black American kids are killed by the police than white kids. Another song is "Black or White" by Michael Jackson, pleading for the conviction that the colour and race of human beings do not matter ("I said if you're thinkin' of being my brother, it don't matter if you're black or white."). This video is particularly interesting because it uses a special technique which changes (or morphs) one image into another through a seamless transition (morphing technique).

Chapter 4

1.

Frith: surface meaning, intended meaning, cultural / ideological meaning

2.

individual answers

3.

pro: original idea, heart-moving story, snowman as universal Christmas motif, clip can trigger lively discussions ...
con: little language input, rather long, kitchy ...
The *making of* clip gives interesting background information in easy-to-understand English.

Chapter 5

1.

sketch: an elaborated and dramatised joke, a brief scene – *sketch comedy*: a series of short sketches – *skit*: a light dramatized joke (*sketch*: more ambitious)

2.

task 8: customer's strategies: using various expressions for "dead", trying to wake up the parrot, shouting at it, banging it against the counter, lettting it fall to the floor, becoming more impatient
shopkeeper's strategies: trying to avoid contact ("We're closing for lunch"), referring to outward appearance ("beautiful plumage"), manipulating objects (jogging the cage), putting forward silly arguments (resting, stunned, pining for the fiords, kipping on its back, nailed because of its strength)
task 9: word field 'to die'

Register			
Legal	*Religious*	*Theatre*	*General*
has ceased to be, is a late parrot, it has passed on, has expired	has gone to meet its maker, bereft of life, rests in peace, has joined the choir invisible	has rung down the curtain	is no more, is pushing up the daisies, is a stiff, is an ex-parrot

Task 10a): answers may vary – absurd situation, characters' behaviour, ways of arguing, mixing different registers and sociolects, word field 'to die'

3.

individual answers

Chapter 6

1.

1. situation, 2. TV, 3. Simpsons, 4. setting, 5. cliff-(hanger), 6. running, 7. audience, 8. popular, 9. 30, 10. seasons, 11. wit, 12. mass.

2.

individual answers

3.

individual answers

Chapter 7

1.

videos (Snap TV), CD-ROMs, (Wizadora), educational videoportals (Planet Schule), general websites (BBC), commercial videosellers (LinguaVideo: documentary on The Life and Works of William Shakespeare)

2.

individual answers

3.

pro: professionally crafted product, conversational American English, easy to understand, sitcom-style story-lines, pre-viewing questions, language focus sections on vocabulary / idioms / pronunciation / grammar, helpful teachers' manuals ...

con: a bit old (1990s), overly repetitive structure of language exercises, age of protagonists (only a few teenagers), American production style ...

Chapter 8

1.

pros: natural, entertaining, simple
cons: passive consumption? implicit learning? teachers' professional reputation?

2.

e. g. Group 1: Action, story and plot
Action refers to what happens in a film. It may be in verbal or non-verbal form. One can also distinguish between external action, i.e. action that is visible because it happens in the outside world, and internal action, i.e. emotions and thoughts.
Action is woven into a *story*, i.e. the chronological sequence of events. A story can be structured into different forms of *plot*. As in a written story, a film plot often falls into an exposition (opening), rising action, climax, falling action, dénouement, end – and the credits. The opening is very important as it sets the scene, introduces the main characters, hints at the theme, raises suspense, and gets the story going. At the centre of the film there is often a conflict in which the main characters are involved. The film may have a happy ending, a sad (tragic) ending or an open ending.

3.

individual answers

Chapter 9

1.

pros: combining viewing and working, Balanced Teaching, applying the PWP pattern

cons: fragmentation of the film, unnatural viewing mode, much classroom time needed

2.

a)

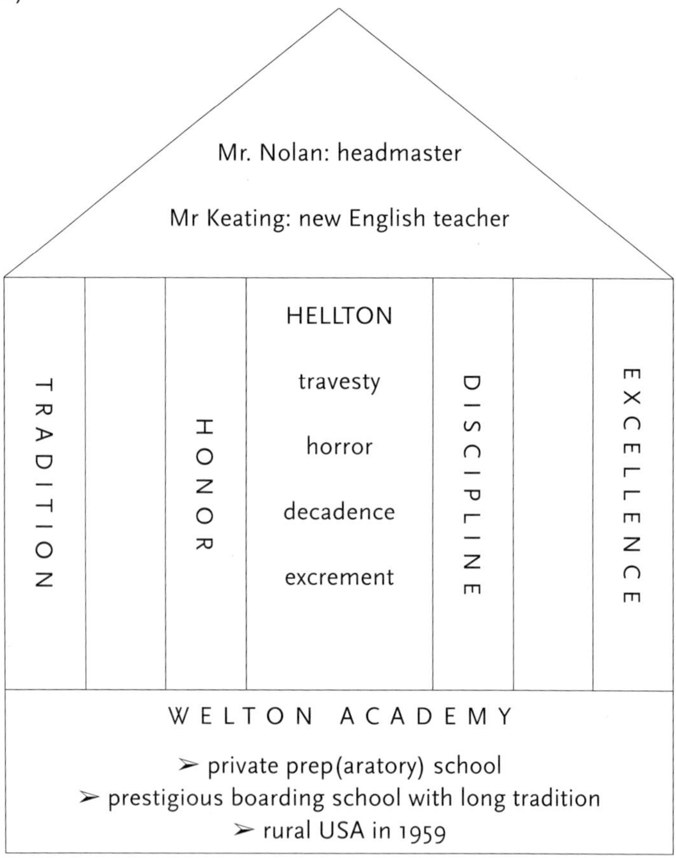

b) 1. parallel to boys on the staircase: noisy, wild, starting something new, breaking free
2. other teachers as *foils* to Mr Keating, to emphasize how different Keating is, to direct the viewers' sympathies to Keating

3. strange, spooky – mysterious sound, old photos, camera angle (from behind pupils' backs), Keating's position: behind pupils, whispering – to highlight Keating's unorthodox teaching style and his personality ("different, weird, spooky")
4. contrastive montage: talking, action vs silence, loneliness (Todd) – to highlight Todd's problem
5. visual (countryside) and musical (harp music) beauty/romanticism foreshadow the following love scene

3.

individual answers

Chapter 10

1.

pros: gain in time, setting priorities, viewing and working ...
cons: fragmentation, distortion, lack of understanding ......

2.

a) Deleted scenes
Worksheet 1
1. Jesus did.
2. He is a beggar and asks them for money.
3. He has lost his livelihood.
4. He was a Roman ... soldier.
5. He gets furious and does not accept being a Roman.
Worksheet 2:
1. True
2. False. The three Magi ..... recognized their mistake.
3. False. It was a stoning, and the man had used the word "Jehovah".
4. False. He sold animal titbits at the amphitheatre.
5. False. When he was 33 he joined the People's Front of Judea.
6. True
7. True
8. False. ... Pilate's wife ... started fighting against them.
9. True
10. True
Worksheet 3:

1. release, 2. misunderstanding, 3. pulling, 4. pretending, 5. revolutionaries, 6. jolly, 7. suicide, 8. terrific, 9. accuses, 10. cheer

b) Brian Superstar

1. Pre-viewing: *Vocabulary work*

gourd	hard-skinned fleshy fruit of a climbing plant
lilies	a plant growing from a bulb
vow	a solemn promise
heretic	s.o. who does not believe what is generally accepted
juniper	evergreen shrub with dark berries (Wacholder)
bald	having no hair on the scalp

2. Viewing Scenes 16 –18: *Comprehension*

2.1 references to lilies, birds and two servants (cf. Sermon on the Mount)
2.2 first they are puzzled, later they believe he has got a secret
2.3 Brian makes him speak after 18 years of silence
2.4 want to kill him because he does not believe in Brian/the Messiah

3. First viewing of Scene 19: *Finish the statements*

3.1 Mandy insults Judith because she went to bed with her son.
3.2 Judith explains ... by claiming that Brian is a born leader.
3.3 Brian tells them that they are individuals and should think for themselves.

4. Second viewing of Scene 19

4.1 "Look, you've got it all wrong. You don't need to ***follow*** me. You don't need to follow ***anybody***. You've got to think for ***yourselves***. You're all ***individuals***."
"You're all ***different***."
"Well, that's it. You've all got to ***work*** it ***out*** for yourselves."
4.2 ignorance, misunderstanding Brian's message, discrepancy between their words and behaviour ("We're all individuals" spoken in chorus), Dennis as a funny dissident ("I'm not")

5. Analysis: *Satirical intention*

"Don't pass judgement ...: tendency "to judge a sausage by its skin", intolerance, discrimination of "otherness"
In no time, Brian has a crowd ...: herd instinct, the masses' need of leaders, religious fanatism, power of (status) symbols
The crowd believes Brian ...: gullibility, belief in supernatural events, irrationality

They want to kill Simon ...: violence, killing in the name of God (N. Ireland), group pressure, persecution of religious / ethnic / political outsiders
Brian – Judith – Mandy – crowd: star – groupie – manager – fans: star cult
"Yes, we're all individuals." – "Yes, we are all different": individuality vs conformity, thinking vs following, talking vs acting

3.
Individual answers

Chapter 11

1.

pros: focus, time, flexibility ...
cons: decontextualisation, distortion, loss of suspense ...

2.

group 1 (setting): time: a sunny summer's day in 1981 → cheerful atmosphere; place: a bus stop with a bench near a city park → waiting for a bus to travel somewhere
group 2 (suspense): What does the feather symbolize? Who is the protagonist? Why is he waiting at the bus stop? Is he stupid? What does the box of chocolates stand for?
group 3 (protagonist): worn-out sports shoes, short haircut, long trousers, chequered shirt (neat, but not fashionable?); monologue, strange intonation, speaks with his mouth full (mentally retarded?); stiff posture, twitching eyes, unsteady glance (insecure?), at the end: frowning with closed eyes (remembering a childhood scene?)
group 4 (symbolism): feather in the wind (hero driven by fate?), worn-out shoes (hard life?), suitcase (stages in his life?), box of chocolates (Mom? destiny?)
group 5 (camera): two long shots with one cut in between (feather, slow pace), close-up (shoes), tilt upward (hero), zoom out into a long static shot (link between feather / shoes and protagonist)
group 6 (sound): piano solo, then strings (slow, melodious), noise of the wind (nostalgic atmosphere, bitter-sweet memories)

3.

pros: focus on viewing, reduction of decoding load, stimulus for speaking and creating activities, change in classroom methodology, here: father's accent hard to understand, cursing (end of the clip) ... cons: no language input, English accent withheld, chance of working on language awareness (regiolects) wasted ...

Chapter 12

1.

Novel: Margaret Atwood's The Handmaid's Tale (1990, dir. V. Schlöndorff)
Play: Arthur Miller's Death of a Salesman (1985, starring D. Hoffman)
Short story: Roddy Doyle's New Boy (2007, dir. Steph Green)
Poem: E.A. Poe's The Raven (1963, dir. Roger Corman)
Picture book: Jeff Kinney's Diary of a Wimpy Kid (dir. Thor Freudenthal, 2010)

2.

individual answers

3.

individual answers

Chapter 13

1.

orality, reception before production, multisensory learning, clarity, playful learning, in small steps ...

2.

individual answers

3.

pros: authentic material, pupils get used to English sounds, fun, change of methods, repetitive patterns, stories, visual scaffolding ...

cons: language too difficult, lack of appropriate material to bridge the content – language gap ...

Chapter 14

1.

listening-viewing comprehension: e. g. multiple choice, film analysis: e. g. viewing grid, evaluation: e. g. film review, creation: e. g. making a film magazine

2.

Test 2
Q 1: summary: see synopsis, linking: Beginning and end form a circle by focusing on the same person, i.e. Todd. But whereas at first Todd feels desperate about not being able to write a suitable poem, at the end he can be happy because he has overcome his shyness.
Q 2: Medium shots and close-ups of Keating emphasize his function as a role model.
Whitman's wall picture from a low angle stresses his importance: "I sound my barbaric yawp over the rooftops of the world" (blackboard).
At the beginning when Todd is unable to speak the camera is rather static.
With Keating's help, Todd gradually dares to speak out; the camera moves across the classroom very fast, reflecting Todd's agitated mood.
Q 3: Creative, student-centred assignment (writing one's own poem)
Open teaching style
Personal and constructive evaluation of the various poems (praising, encouraging, criticizing)
Cynical remark towards Mr Hopkins ("Congratulations, Mr Hopkins, you have the first poem that has a negative score on the Pritchard scale.")
Rejection of a formalistic and academic approach to poetry (anti-Pritchard)
Ability to inspire and influence students
Q 4: Todd: This morning I had my worst and best English lesson. We had to read out our poems, and Keating picked me, of course. First I couldn't ...But then .....

Mr Hopkins: I'm so cool. I really am. "The cat sat on the mat." That's the poem I read out in Keating's class today. All the boys grinned. Only Keating said it was ordinary.....
Knox: Oh Chris! I love you. Do you like this poem? I read it out in class today, and Keating thought it was fine – because it's about love – and that's a major theme in life and poetry. I'm not sure if you .....

Test 3
Q 1:
– before: Brian arrested but granted release by Pilate, crucifixion party
– after: Mr Frisbee trying to cheer up Brian, final song
Q 2:
2.1 - Gregory: feels entitled to be crucified in a purely Jewish area, Samaritans not wanted
– saintly passer-by: not his cross, was holding it for someone else
2.2 - PFJ: greetings to Brian on the occasion of his martyrdom, singing "For he's a jolly good fellow"
– JPF: committing suicide
– Judith: thanking him for his terrific deed
– Mandy: accusing him of being ungrateful to her
– similar reactions: do not help/rescue him
Q 3:
– involved in preparing and reading pretentious statements on behalf of their movement, abstaining from acting
– gap between word and deed, people taking themselves too seriously
Q 4: e.g.
– Gregory's insistence on formal aspects (Jewish section) in the face of death
– Mr Cheeky's optimistic and cheerful attitude despite bleak prospects
– PFJ's silly behaviour
– JPF: committing suicide to frighten the Romans
– mass crucifixion

Q 5:
a) yes: parallels between Brian and Jesus

no: criticism of religious intolerance/fanatism and political stupidity, no attack on Jesus Christ, fundamentalists' furor based on lack of knowledge
b) a lot of parallels, e.g. birth in a cowshed, sermon on the mount, dedicated followers, preaching, Pilate, crucifixion
c) no: may hurt the feelings of deeply religious pupils, problems with listening comprehension
yes: funny film, interesting topics, current relevance, cultural studies, practice in various language skills

3.

individual answers

Chapter 15

1.

purpose (between intensive listening-viewing and listening-viewing for gist), place (between classroom teaching and learning outside the classroom), activities (tasks and exercises), goal (learning and enjoying) ...

2.

individual answers

3.

individual answers

Bibliography

A

Abraham, U. *Filme im Deutschunterricht.*
2009 | Stuttgart: Klett

Aitken, I. (Ed.) *Encyclopedia of the Documentary Film.*
2005 | New York: Routledge

Ambrose, D. *Finding New Messages in Television Commercials.*
2002 | In: English Teaching Forum Online 40/2
http://exchanges.state.gov/forum/vols/vol40/no2/p44.htm
(13.01.2013)

Anderson, A.
Lynch, T. *Listening.*
1995 | Oxford: Oxford University Press

Antor, H. (Ed.) *Shakespeare alternativ.*
1997 | Themenheft Der Fremdsprachliche Unterricht Englisch, 6

Aufderheide, P. *Documentary Film: A Very Short Introduction.*
2007 | Oxford: Oxford University Press

B

Bachtin, M. *Die Ästhetik des Wortes.*
1979 | Frankfurt a.M.: Suhrkamp

Baddock, B. *Getting in the Scene: Film in the Language Class.*
1990 | In: Praxis des Neusprachlichen Unterrichts 37, pp. 145–153

Baddock, B. *Using Films in the English Class.*
1996 | Hertfordshire: Phoenix ELT

Baker, J. *Teaching TV Sitcom.*
2003 | London: bfi

Ballstaedt, S. *Integrative Verarbeitung bei audio-visuellen Medien.*
1987 | Tübingen: DIFF, Forschungsberichte 46

Blell, G.
Luetge, C. *Sehen, Hören, Verstehen und Handeln: Filme im Fremdsprachenunterricht.*
2004 | In: PRAXIS Fremdsprachenunterricht, 6, pp. 402–405, 445

Boggs, J. / Petrie, D. *The Art of Watching Films (with Tutorial DVD).* 2008 | New York: McGraw-Hill

Branigan, E. *Narrative Comprehension and Film.* 1992 | London: Routledge

Bredella, L. *Der amerikanische Dokumentarfilm: Zugang zur amerikanischen Wirklichkeit?* 1994 | In: Bredella, L. / Lenz, G., Der amerikanische Dokumentarfilm: Herausforderungen für die Didaktik, Tübingen: Narr, pp. 81 – 107

Bredella, L. *'Bend It like Beckham': Überlegungen zu einer rezeptionsästhetischen Filmdidaktik.* 2004 | In: Der Fremdsprachliche Unterricht Englisch 68, pp. 28 – 32

Burwitz-Melzer, E. *Ice Age: ein Zeichentrickfilm in der Sekundarstufe I.* 2004 | In: Der fremdsprachliche Unterricht Englisch, 68, pp. 14 – 19

C

Carle, E. *The Very Hungry Caterpillar.* www.dailymotion.com/video/xheay8_the-very-hungry-caterpillar_animals#.USuWDR1WySo (26.02.2013)

Cartmell, D. 100+ *Years of Adaptations, or, Adaptation as the Art Form of Democracy.* 2012 | In: Cartmell, D. (ed.), A Companion to Literature, Film, and Adaptation, Malden: Wiley-Blackwell, pp. 1 – 13

Chee, H. *Anregungen zur sprachlichen Reaktivierung und Textauswertung am Beispiel eines Werbetextes in der Jahrgangsstufe 11.* 1994 | In: Die neueren Sprachen 93/6, pp. 154 – 164

Cooper, R. / Lavery, M. / Rinvolucri, M. *Video.* 1991 | Oxford: Oxford University Press

COUNCIL OF EUROPE (ED.) *Common European Framework of Reference for Languages: Learning, Teaching, Assessment.*
2001 | Cambridge: Cambridge University Press

D

DASENBROCK, C. LUETGE, C. *Viewing. (Series: Teaching Skills. Kompetenztraining in der gymnasialen Oberstufe, mit DVD).*
2013 | Berlin: Cornelsen.

DAVIS, R. *TV Commercial Messages: An Untapped Video Resource for Content-Based Classes.*
1997 | In: The Language Teacher Online.
http://jalt-publications.org/tlt/files/97/mar/davis.html (01.12.2005)

DECKE-CORNILL, H. *'Story of a Beautiful Country': Ein Dokumentarfilm aus dem Neuen Alten Südafrika.*
2009 | In: Leitzke-Ungerer, E. (ed.), pp. 327 – 342

DIXON, W. FOSTER, G. *A Short History of Film.*
2008 | New Jersey: Rutgers University Press

DOYE, C. *Films for Self Study.*
1998 | In: Modern English Teacher 4, pp. 60 – 63

DUEWEL, D. VON DER GRUEN, J. *Soap Operas in the Classroom – a Contribution to Media Literacy, (I), (II).*
2001 | In: Fremdsprachenunterricht 2, pp. 94 – 106

DUNLEAVY, T. *Television Drama: Form, Agency, Innovation.*
2009 | Basingstoke: Palgrave Macmillan

DYER, R. *Film Studies: Critical Approaches.*
2000 | Oxford: Oxford University Press

E

EINHOFF, K. *Power Pack English – Media Literacy. Practising Listening and Viewing Skills.*
2011 | Paderborn: Schöningh

Ellis, J.
McLane, B.
A New History of Documentary Film.
2005 | New York: Continuum International

Erdmenger, M.
Neue Medien: Video und Computer als Handlungs-,Partner'?
1989 | In: Bach, G. / Timm, J. (ed.), Englischunterricht, Tübingen: Francke, pp. 128 – 160

Europarat (ed.)
Gemeinsamer europäischer Referenzrahmen für Sprachen: Lernen, lehren, beurteilen.
2001 | Berlin: Langenscheidt

F

Fraser, P.
Teaching Music Videos.
2005 | London: BFI Education

Fraser, P.
Oram, B.
Teaching Digital Video Production.
2004 | London: British Film Institute

Frenken, W. et al.
American Beauty.
2001 | Paderborn: Schöningh

Frith, K.
Undressing the Ad: Reading Culture in Advertising.
1998 | Frankfurt: Lang

G

Gallacher, L.
Video and Young Learners 1.
2003 | Teaching English / British Council / BBC. 4 www.teachin-genglish.org.uk/articles/video-young-lear
(26.02.13)

Giddings, R.
Selby, K.
Wensley, C.
Screening the Novel. The Theory and Practice of Literary Dramatization.
1990 | Houndmills: Macmillan

Grau, M.
Indien im Film: 'Monsoon Wedding'.
2004 | In: Der Fremdsprachliche Unterricht Englisch 68, pp. 34 – 39

Grimm, N.
'The Corporation': Zum reflektiert-kritischen Einsatz von Dokumentarfilmen im Englischunterricht.
2009 | In: Leitzke-Ungerer, E. (ed.), pp. 343 – 358

Grindhammer, L. *Hollywood in the English Language Classroom: The Dead Poets' Society.*
1993 | In: Neusprachliche Mitteilungen aus Wissenschaft und Praxis, 4, pp. 244 – 250

Gruenewald, A. *Sehen und Verstehen: Analyse referenzsemantischer Zeichen in Spielfilmen.*
2009 | In: Leitzke-Ungerer, E. (ed.), pp. 221 – 240

Gunzenhaeuser, R.
Hahn, A. *Sitcoms und Pragmatik.*
2009 | In: Leitzke-Ungerer (ed.), pp. 419 – 431

Gymnich, M. *A Commitment Phobic, a 12-Year-Old, and a Dead Duck: About a Boy.*
2004 | In: Der Fremdsprachliche Unterricht Englisch 68, pp. 20 – 26

H

Hallet, W.
Königs, F.G. *Handbuch Fremdsprachendidaktik.*
2010 | Seelze-Velber: Friedrich

Hartmann, U. *Rabbit-Proof Fence.*
2006 | Paderborn: Schöningh

Hecke, C. *Bilder im Fremdsprachenunterricht: Neue Ansätze, Kompetenzen und Methoden.*
2010 | Tübingen: Narr

Hedge, T. *Teaching and Learning in the English Language Classroom.*
2000 | Oxford: Oxford University Press

Henseler, R.
Möller, S.
Surkamp, C. *Filme im Englischunterricht – Grundlagen, Methoden, Genre.*
2011 | Seelze: Kallmeyer

Hescher, A. *Racism, Intercultural Encounters and Politcial Correctness in Metin Hüseyin's Film 'Anita and Me'. A Didactic Approach.*
2009 | In: Leitzke-Ungerer, E. (ed.), pp. 117 – 136

Holden, W. *Making the Most of Movies: Keeping Film Response Journals.*
2000 | In: Modern English Teacher 2, pp. 40 – 46

Hutcheon, L. *A Theory of Adaptation.*
2006 | New York: Routledge

J

Johnson, S. *Everything Bad Is Good for You.*
2005 | New York: Riverhead

K

Kaiser, M. *New Approaches to Exploiting Film in the Foreign Language Classroom.*
2011 | In: L2 Journal, 3/2
http://escholarship.org/uc/item/6568p4f4 (27.02.2013)

Karasek, H. *Mein Kino.*
1994 | Hamburg: Hoffmann und Campe

Keazor, H. / Wuebbena, T *Video Thrills the Radio Star: Musikvideos – Geschichte, Themen, Analysen.*
2007 | Bielefeld: Transcript Verlag

Kelen, C. *Television Commercials: Texts with Big Potential for Language Learning.*
1991 | In: Language Teacher 15/10, pp. 9 – 12

Kieweg, W. *Mentale Prozesse beim Hörverstehen.*
2003 | In: Der Fremdsprachliche Unterricht Englisch 64/64, pp. 18 – 22

Kieweg, W. et al. (ed.) *Der Fremdsprachliche Unterricht Englisch*
2003 | Themenheft Hörverstehen 64-65

KMK (ed.) *Bildungsstandards für die erste Fremdsprache (Englisch / Französisch) für den Mittleren Schulabschluss.*
2004 | München: Wolters Kluwer

Knobloch, H. / Raab, J. *Der Werbespot als kommunikative Gattung.*
2002 | In: Willems, H. (ed.), Die Gesellschaft der Werbung, Wiesbaden: Verlag für Sozialwissenschaften, pp. 139 – 154

Konigsberg, I. *The Complete Film Dictionary.*
1997 | London: Penguin

Kreis, R. *Videos im Englischunterricht der Grundschule.*
2004 | In: Fremdsprachen Frühbeginn, 1, pp. 41 – 49

Kreuzer, H. *Arten der Literaturadaption.*
1993 | In: Gast, W. (ed.), Literaturverfilmung, Bamberg: C.C. Buchners Verlag, pp. 28 – 31

Kuechler, U. *Screening the Green, Greening the Screen: Umweltfilme im Fremdsprachenunterricht.*
2009 | In: Leitzke-Ungerer, E. (ed.), pp. 359 – 378

L

Landesbildstelle Suedbayern (ed.) *Schülerzentrierte Methoden zur Auswertung von Filmen im Unterricht.*
2000 | www.labio1.rz.fh-muenchen/mpaed/artikel/filmausw/filmauswert/html (15.12.2012)

Landesinstitut fuer Schulentwicklung Baden-Wuerttemberg (ed.) *Bildungsplan Gymnasium.*
2004 | www.schule-bw.de/unterricht/bildungsstandards/ (28.12.2012)

Leitch, T. *Adaptation and Intertextuality, or, What Isn't an Adaptation, and What Does It Matter?*
2012 | In: Cartmell, D. (ed.), A Companion to Literature, Film, and Adaptation, Malden: Wiley-Blackwell, pp. 87 – 104

Leitzke-Ungerer, E. (ed.) *Film im Fremdsprachenunterricht. Literarische Stoffe, interkulturelle Ziele, mediale Wirkung.*
2009 | Stuttgart: ibidem

Liebelt, W. (ed.). *Der Film 'Dead Poets Society' im Englischunterricht. Arbeitshilfen, Filmkritiken, Aufsätze.*
1995 | In: Materialien zur Medienpädagogik, 6/1

Lütge, C. *Mit Filmen Englisch unterrichten.*
2012 | Berlin: Cornelsen

M

McFarlane, B. *Novel to Film. An Introduction to the Theory of Adapation.*
1996 | Oxford: Clarendon Press

Massler, U. *Adidas, Nike und Pepsi: Football Commercials im Netz und im Fremdsprachenunterricht.*
2006 | In: Thaler, E. (ed.), Fußball – Fremdsprachen – Forschung, Aachen: Shaker, pp. 135 – 147

Mindt, D. / Schlüter, N. *Englisch in den Klassen 3 und 4 – Grundlagen für einen ergebnisorientierten Unterricht.*
2003 | Berlin: Cornelsen

Monaco, J. *How to Read a Film.*
2009 | Oxford: Oxford University Press

Mueller, B. *Der Mist wird besser.*
2006 | In: Süddeutsche Zeitung 08.08.2006, p. 14

N

Nold, G. / Steffenhagen, A. *'Have You Met Miss Jones'? – Eine authentische Begegnung mit Literatur und Film im Fremdsprachenunterricht.*
2004 | In: Müller-Hartmann, A. / Schocker-von Ditfurth, M. (ed.), Aufgabenorientierung im Fremdsprachenunterricht. Task-based Language Learning and Teaching. Tübingen: Narr, pp. 257 – 273

P

Phillips, S. *Young Learners.*
1995 | Oxford: Oxford University Press

Picken, J. *State of the Ad: The Role of Advertisements in EFL Teaching.*
1999 | In: ELT Journal 53/4, pp. 249 – 255

Planet Schule *Teens in South Africa: Michael – Life is Football.*
2013 | www.planet-schule.de/sf/php/02_sen01.php?sendung=7910
(27.02.2013)

Planet Schule *Teens in South Africa: Nandipha between Dancefloor and Township.* 2013 | www.planet-schule.de/sf/php/02_sen01.php?sendung=7911 (27.02.2013)

Poppe, S. *Visualität in Literatur und Film: Eine medienkomparatistische Untersuchung moderner Erzähltexte und ihrer Verfilmungen.* 2007 | Göttingen: Vandenhoeck

Porsch, R. Grotjahn, R. Tesch, B. *Hörverstehen und Hör-Sehverstehen in der Fremdsprache – unterschiedliche Konstrukte?* 2010 | In: Zeitschrift für Fremdsprachenforschung (ZFF), 2, pp. 143 – 189

R

Rokoszewska, K. *Comparing Selected Modern Methods of Teaching English to Young Learners.* 2011 | Frankfurt am Main: Peter Lang

Rost, M. *Introducing Listening.* 1994 | Harmondsworth: Penguin

S

Schmidt, K. *Japanese TV Ads: A Video Resource for the English Discussion Class.* 1998 | http://jalt-publications.org/tlt/files/98/aug/sh_schmidt.html. (01.12.2005)

Schmidt, S. *Wortschatzerwerb beim Fernsehen.* 1998 | Frankfurt am Main: Lang

Schwerdtfeger, I. *Übungen zum Hör-Seh-Verstehen.* 2003 | In: Bausch, K. / Christ, H. / Krumm, H. (ed.), Handbuch Fremdsprachenunterricht. Tübingen: Francke, pp. 299 – 302

Scott, A. O. *Introduction.* 2004 | In: Nichols, P. (ed.), The New York Times Guide to the Best 1,000 Movies Ever Made, St. Martin's Griffin www.nytimes.com/ref/movies/1000bestintro.html (18.03.2013)

Schumann, A. *Interkulturelles Lernen mit Filmen im Fremdsprachenunterricht.*
2009 | In: Leitzke-Ungerer, E. (ed.), pp. 171 – 186

Simon, J. *Wirkungen von Daily Soaps auf Jugendliche.*
2006 | München: Reinhard Fischer

Snell, J. *Schema Theory and the Humour of 'Little Britain'.*
2006 | In: English Today, 1, pp. 59 – 64

Sherman, J. *Using Authentic Video in the Language Classroom.*
2003 | Cambridge: Cambridge University Press

Spitzer, M. *Vorsicht Bildschirm! Elektronische Medien, Gehirnentwicklung, Gesundheit und Gesellschaft.*
2006 | München: DTV

Staatsinstitut fuer Schulqualitaet und Bildungsforschung *Time to Talk.*
2005 | Berlin: Cornelsen

Stam, R. *Introduction: The Theory and Practice of Adaptation.*
2005 | In: Stam, R. / Raengo, A. (ed.), Literature and Film. A Guide to the Theory and Practice of Film Adaptation, Malden: Blackwell, pp. 1 – 52

Stempleski, S. Tomalin, B. *Video in Action.*
1989 | London: Longman

Stempleski, S. Tomalin, B. *Film.*
2001 | Oxford: Oxford University Press

Stiller, H. *Texte und ihre Verfilmungen. Vorteile einer Medienkombination für das textverarbeitende Lerngespräch im fortgeschrittenen Englischunterricht.*
1990 | In: Der Fremdsprachliche Unterricht Englisch 99, pp. 4 – 9

Surkamp, C. (ed.) *Der Fremdsprachliche Unterricht Englisch*
2004 | Themenheft Teaching Films, 68

Surkamp, C. *Literaturverfilmungen im Unterricht: Die Perspektive der Fremdsprachendidaktik.*
2009 | In: Leitzke-Ungerer, E. (ed.), pp. 61 – 80

Surkamp, C. *Close-up: Exploring the Language of Film (DVD-ROM).*
2010 | Paderborn: Schöningh

T

Tepe, T. (ed.) *Filmanalyse. Vorschläge für Klausuren und Klassenarbeiten.*
2004 | Stuttgart: Klett

Thaler, E. *Musikvideoclips im Englischunterricht.*
1999 | München: Langenscheidt

Thaler, E. *EinFach Englisch: Monty Python. Unterrichtsmodell.*
2000 | Paderborn: Schöningh

Thaler, E. *DVD im Englischunterricht.*
2001 | In: Der Fremdsprachliche Unterricht Englisch, 53, pp. 40 – 41

Thaler, E. *Dead Poets Society.*
2003 | Paderborn: Schöningh

Thaler, E. *Popular Culture.*
2005 | Paderborn: Schöningh

Thaler, E. *The Trend's Your 'Friends' – Methoden zur Arbeit mit TV-Sitcoms.*
2005 | In: Der Fremdsprachliche Unterricht Englisch, 75, pp. 36 – 37

Thaler, E. *Offene Lernarrangements im Englischunterricht.*
2007 | München: Langenscheidt

Thaler, E. *Film-based Language Learning.*
2007 | In: PRAXIS Fremdsprachenunterricht, 1, pp. 9 – 14

Thaler, E. *Hör-Seh-Verstehen.*
2007 | In: PRAXIS Fremdsprachenunterricht, 4, pp. 14 – 19

Thaler, E. (ed.) *The New Summit. Lehrwerk für die Oberstufe.*
2007 | Paderborn: Schöningh

Thaler, E. *Internet-Videos – Fremdsprachenlernen für die YouTube-Generation.*
2008 | In: PRAXIS Fremdsprachenunterricht 1, pp. 14 – 18

Thaler, E. *Shakespeares Hamlet intermedial.*
2008 | In: Ahrens, R. et al. (ed.), Moderne Dramendidaktik für den Englischunterricht, Heidelberg: Winter, pp. 339 – 352

Thaler, E. *Lernerfolg durch Balanced Teaching.*
2010 | Berlin: Cornelsen

Thaler, E. *Film-based Language Learning – im und außerhalb des Klassenzimmers.*
2010 | In: Gehring, W. / Stinshoff, E. (ed.), Außerschulische Lernorte des Fremdsprachenunterrichts, Braunschweig: Bildungshaus Schulbuchverlage, pp. 105 – 112

Thaler, E. *Literal Music Videos*
2010 | In: PRAXIS Fremdsprachenunterricht 4, p. 3

Thaler, E. *Englisch unterrichten.*
2012 | Berlin: Cornelsen

Tomalin, B. *Video in the English Class.*
1990 | London: BBC

U

Underwood, M. *Teaching Listening.*
1994 | London: Longman

W

Waas, L. / Hamm, W. *Englischunterricht in der Grundschule konkret.*
2004 | Donauwörth: Auer

Wagner, G. *The Novel and the Cinema*
1975 | Rutherford: Fairleigh Dickinson University Press

Weissling, H. Yareham, B. *Video-Ideen für den Englischunterricht.* 2001 | Berlin: Cornelsen

Williamson, J. Jill, V. *Film is Content: A Study Guide for the Advanced ESL Classroom.* 1996 | University of Michigan Press

Wood, D. *Film Communication Theory and Practice in Teaching English as a Foreign Language.* 1995 | Lewiston: Edwin Mellen Press

Z

Zane Education *The Benefits of Using Video in Education.* 2013 | www.zaneeducation.com/education-and-video.php (23.02.2013)

Zerweck, B. *Filmanalyse und Cultural Studies: US-amerikanische Kulturthemen in 'The Big Lebowski' und amerikanischen Vietnamfilmen.* 2004 | In: Der Fremdsprachliche Unterricht Englisch, 68, pp. 40 – 45

Bildnachweis

Abb. 1 Holger Ellgaard: Bell & Howell Stummfilmprojektor "Filmo 129" från 1934, 2007
lizensiert unter Creative Commons

Abb. 2 Dinner for One oder Der 90. Geburtstag (Dinner for one, GB 1963, Regie Heinz Dunkhase) Freddie Frinton, May Warden.
No: 00096479.000 Date: 25.11.1998, Cinetext Bildarchiv

Abb. 3 Alicia Keys
No: 00145794, Date: 15.01.2002, Cinetext Bildarchiv

Abb. 4 Gage Skidmore: Bart Simpson statue, 2010
lizensiert unter Creative Commons

Abb. 5 Daniel Schwen: Looking south from Top of the Rock, New York City, 2005
lizensiert unter Creative Commons

Abb. 6 Foto: chensiyuan: times square night 2013 new york city manhattan, 2013
lizensiert unter Creative Commons

Abb. 7 How I Met Your Mother (TV-Serie, USA 2005) Alyson Hannigan, Jason Segel, Josh Radner, Cobie Smulders, Neil Patrick Harris
No: 00672508, Cinetext/Allstar/20th CentFox TV

Abb. 8 Bowling For Columbine (CDN/USA 2002, Regie: Michael Moore)
No: 00186144, Date: 20.11.2002, Credit: Cinetext Bildarchiv

Abb. 9 Forrest Gump (USA 1994, Regie: Robert Zemeckis) Tom Hanks, Filmposter
No: 00132989.000, Cinetext/Richter

Abb. 10 Der Club der toten Dichter (Dead Poets Society, USA 1989, Regie: Peter Weir) Dylan Kussman, Robert Sean Leonard, Robin Williams, Allelon Ruggiero
No: 00046141.000, Cinetext Bildarchiv

Abb. 11 Das Leben des Brian (Life of Brian, GB 1979, Regie: Terry Jones) Michael Palin, Terence Bayler, Terry Jones, Graham Chapman, Eric Idle
No: 00218680, Cinetext Bildarchiv

Abb. 12 Billy Elliot (Billy Elliot – I will dance, GB 2000, Regie: Stephen Daldry) Jamie Bell

No: 00090716.000, Date: 25.08.2000, Cinetext Bildarchiv

Abb. 13 Wallace & Gromit: Auf der Jagd nach dem Riesenkaninchen (Wallace & Gromit: The Curse Of The Were-Rabbit, GB 2005, Regie: Steve Box, Nick Park)
No: 00305013 VIP/Cinetext